HOW TO PREACH FOR
FOR
REVIVAL

E. A. JOHNSTON

COVER PHOTOS:

See the description on the back cover of the book.

DEDICATION

The following chapters are dedicated to the memory of Clem Dear of Oak Park, Illinois, who gave me my first job in his Bible Book Store, gave me my first Bible, and led me to Jesus because he wouldn't let a thirteen year-old-boy go to Hell.

TABLE OF CONTENTS

PREFACE

In the book of Amos in chapter eight and verse eleven we read: *"Behold, the days come, saith the Lord GOD, that I will send a famine in the land, not a famine of bread, nor a thirst for water, but of hearing the words of the LORD."*

Is this not the day in which we live? In our pulpits across the land very little preaching takes place, it is mainly teaching. Teaching informs, preaching transforms. And much of the preaching that is taking place is anemic, lacking power and sound doctrine. Not only is there a famine of hearing the word of God, there is a famine of preachers!

My homiletical mentor, Dr. Stephen F. Olford, taught me expository preaching, but we need more than just that in this late hour of the Last Days where the spirit of Antichrist is already in the land. We need a return to the searching sermons of the Puritans, which were full of sound doctrine and resonating with power from on high! This is a book on how to preach for revival and the salvation of souls.

CHAPTER ONE
NEEDED: PREACHERS

"Why are the preachers in the Book of Acts turning the world upside down? Why aren't our preachers today turning the world upside down? Because the dissimilarities are obvious"

E. A. Johnston

Years ago, I was asked to do a radio interview on Christian radio and the female moderator related the following story to me.

She said that she once had a job that was eye opening in regard to ministry. She said she was hired by an organization to conduct a religious poll on the ministry and her job was to randomly telephone pastors around the country and ask them the following question, "Why did you become a pastor?" She told me that she contacted 1,000 ministers all across America and she was shocked by their answers as to why they entered the ministry. She related that one man said he became a pastor because he was a single man and he wanted to meet women! Another man said, that he was gifted with a winning personality that attracted crowds so that is why he became a pastor. Another man said, he wanted to be a help the downtrodden in his community, so he thought the best way to do that was to become a pastor of church. One man said he was a good public speaker so this occupation best fit his talent. Another man said he had graduated seminary and earned a doctor degree and so this was his reason for becoming a minister because he was properly educated. This radio host told me that after speaking to hundreds and hundreds of ministers across the country they each had a reason to become a minister and it mostly self-motivated. Out of the 1,000 men contacted, only one man, she told me, had a different answer from all the rest. He was a black pastor in the South and he said the main reason he became a pastor because God called him.

The greatest need in a nation today are: PREACHERS. We need God-called men to take the Word of God and preach the Son of God with an anointing of the Spirit of God. This is the only way we can reach our country for Christ and the gospel.

But preachers need to know how to preach. A seminary training will not make you a preacher. I have graduated from two different seminaries with two doctorate degrees and neither one of those academic institutions taught me how to effectively preach the gospel. I was trained as a preacher by my homiletical mentor, Dr. Stephen F. Olford, of whose expository preaching institute I was in the first graduating class. But even with seminary training and preaching institute training I still had to learn how to preach the Gospel of the Son of God effectively and only the Holy Spirit of God can teach you how to do that!

I will give you an example of the limitations of learning how to preach from a seminary. I was sitting in a preaching class taught by the preaching professor of a big Baptist seminary and one of the students seated next to me raised his hand to ask a question. He said, "I understand Professor what you are saying about communication, and projecting our voices, and annunciating our words clearly—this is all necessary for public speaking but…when I study men whom God has used in former times of revival, men like Jonathan Edwards, I see that the reason God used Jonathan Edwards was because he was a man anointed with the Holy Ghost." The seminary professor gave the student a disgusting look and in a condescending tone he said in a loud voice, "You young man are no Jonathan Edwards!"

I believe that seminary student knew a lot more about preaching than that egg-headed preaching professor! Like I said, you may learn how to be a more effective communicator in seminary but they will not teach you how to preach. This book is handbook to learn how to preach and to preach with power! If you carefully study its chapters and learn its precepts and apply them to your own ministry; I can assure you that you will be a better preacher!

CHAPTER TWO
WE NEED REVIVAL IN OUR PULPITS

"Our only hope today is a revival and reformation in our pulpits across the land. We must cease the madness of continuing with a man-centered gospel that is centered around the happiness of man. And we must return to the God-centered Gospel of our Puritan fathers, and proclaim the sinfulness of man and the holiness of God and the only remedy for sin in the Person of a bloodstained Christ who died for sin!"

E. A. Johnston

Easy believeism has sent multitudes to a Devil's Hell. The "only believe" gospel is a no gospel and it originated from a lost seminary professor who did not believe in repentance as a necessary component to salvation. And he founded a seminary and wrote a systematic theology that has damned millions.

In an effort to grow our church campus through mass evangelism we have adopted man centered methodologies that have corrupted the church and deceived multitudes. The majority pulpits in America teach a man-centered gospel. Jesus came to earth to make your life a little better while you are here and to give you eternal life after you are gone in a place of bliss called heaven. All you have to do is accept him as your personal savior or repeat a prayer or make it public by walking an aisle and we will pat you on the back and say, "Welcome to the family of God!"

We must return to a God-centered gospel, that proclaims the glory of God in the salvation of souls. We must preach a God, who is high and lifted up, whose name is Holy! (Isaiah 57:15). Todays modern evangelism has shrunken God down to man's size, we place God on our level. I heard a seminary trained pastor of a big Baptist church comment: "I can't wait to get to heaven! When I get there I'm gonna walk up to Jesus and grab him by the hand and shake his hand for all he's done for me!"

That is our sad mentality today. This pastor is going to walk up to Jesus like he is a deacon in the hallway at church and glad hand him! I guess that seminary trained pastor never read the scripture in the Book of Revelation where the Apostle John has an encounter with the Risen Christ, and he falls down as dead! We put God on our level today: he thinks like we do, he acts like we do. But God declares,

> *"For my thoughts are not your thoughts, neither are your ways my ways, said the LORD. For as the heavens are higher than the earth, so are my ways higher than your ways, and my thoughts than your thoughts"* (Isaiah 55:8-9).

The prophet Isaiah had a such glimpse of Almighty God that it both startled him and humbled him:

> *"In the year that King Uzziah died: I saw also the Lord sitting upon a throne, high and lifted up, and his train filled the temple. Above it stood the seraphims: each one had six wings; and with twain he covered his face, and with twain he covered his feet, and with twain he did fly. And one cried unto another, and said, Holy, holy, holy, is the LORD of hosts: the whole earth is full of his glory. And the posts of the doors moved at the voice of him that cried, and the house was filled*

with smoke. Then said I, Woe is me! for I am undone; because I am a man of unclean lips, and I dwell in the midst of a people of unclean lips: for mine eyes have seen the King, the LORD of hosts" (Isaiah 6:1-5).

When we preach an exalted view of God then our hearers will see God in all His attributes and recognize their own sinfulness and need of a substitute for sin in the Person of Christ Jesus. But if we preach a gospel that emphasizes the happiness of man, then men will not see themselves as sinners in need of a Savior for sin.

There is a story about an Englishman in the 17th century who traveled from London to Scotland by horse and carriage to hear good preaching. The first Scottish preacher he listened to took for his text Isaiah 57:15,

"For thus saith the high and lofty One that inhabiteth eternity, whose name is Holy; I dwell in the high and holy place, with him also that is of a contrite and humble spirit, to revive the spirit of the humble, and to revive the heart of the contrite ones."

And as the Englishman sat there he saw a big exalted God whose very name is Holy. And this humbled him. The next Scottish preacher he heard, took his text from Jeremiah 17:9,

"The heart is deceitful above all things, and desperately wicked: who can know it?" *And the Englishman said to himself, "*

This man has just showed me the sinfulness and awfulness of my own heart!" The third and last preacher in Scotland he heard on this trip preached a message on the loveliness and preeminence of Christ out of the book of Hebrews. And the Englishman sat spellbound as he reflected on the Christ of the Gospel. On the ride back to London this man reflected on the sermons he had heard: an exalted God, his own wicked heart, and the loveliness of Christ and as he rode through the forest he surrendered his heart to God and received a revealed Christ as his Savior and Lord.

CHAPTER THREE
BLOODY HANDS

"At the Last Judgment there will stand many ministers with bloody hands from their failure to warn men to flee from the wrath to come."

E. A. Johnston

In former days, old time preachers preached that sin was black and Hell was hot, and there was a future judgment that awaited all mankind and every mother's son would stand there on That Day alongside the strictness and severity of God's unbending law, and all will fail that test if they stand there in their own merits for, "All have sinned and come short of the glory of God." One must stand there in the merits of another, The Lord Jesus Christ, the substitute for sin. And they warned their hearers about damnation in a Devil's Hell and that men everywhere should repent or perish. These faithful ministers preached with boldness because they did not fear men but only feared the Almighty. Today we fear our deacons more than God.

In God's Word we see a some startling statements from God that stand out in black print on white paper regarding the sinfulness of man. In Ezekiel 18:4, we read, *"the soul that sinneth it shall die."* Yet, in verse twenty three of the same chapter we read: *"Have I any pleasure at all that the wicked should die? Saith the Lord GOD: and not that he should return from his ways, and live?"*

As a preacher of the gospel this should tell me that it is imperative that all men know that *"the soul that sinneth it shall die"*—meaning perish in an eternal Hell of damnation. We should warn men about their perilous position outside of Christ and without God in the world. That if men die in their sins they surely shall be cast into Hell for all eternity. Alongside of God's justice and wrath (for the sentencing of the law must be carried out upon the guilty, *"I will in no means clear the guilty"*) we must balance the love and mercy of God: *"Have I any pleasure at all that the wicked should die? Saith the Lord GOD: and not that he should return from his ways, and live"*

A preacher aware of these texts sees his clear command to warn men to flee to Christ— their only refuge and remedy for sin. If we fail to warn men about the danger of dying in their sins and facing damnation in a Devil's Hell, then we fail as ministers of the gospel. We clearly see this from God's Word in Ezekiel chapter three and in verses 18-19:

> *"When I say to the wicked, Thou shalt surely die; and thou givest him not warning, nor speakest to warn the wicked from his wicked way, to save his life; the same wicked man shall die in his iniquity but his blood will I require at thine hand. Yet if thou warn the wicked, and he turn not from his wickedness, nor from his wicked way, he shall die in his iniquity; but thou hast delivered thy soul."*

As preachers of the gospel it is imperative that we faithfully handle the Word of God and preach the full counsel of God and warn men of their danger of dying in their sins:

> *"when the Lord Jesus shall be revealed from heaven with his mighty angels, in flaming fire taking vengeance on them that know not God, and that obey not the gospel of our Lord Jesus Christ: who shall be punished with everlasting destruction from the presence of the Lord, and from the glory of his power"* (Second Thessalonians 1:7-9).

There is a big Baptist church in Memphis, Tennessee and one of its former pastors was Dr. R. G. Lee, who preached a famous sermon called, "Payday Someday". There was a member in Dr Lee's congregation, an attorney, who had to be out of town on business frequently, but no matter where this lawyer went he made sure to catch a train back to Memphis on Saturday night so he could listen to R. G. Lee preach on Sunday. He loved to hear that man preach. Well, this lawyer got cancer and he was in the hospital dying and he called for his pastor to come to his bedside. Dr. Lee entered the hospital room whose windows overlooked the Mississippi River. The lawyer told R. G. Lee,

> "I want you to know how much I've enjoyed your preaching through the years and I never missed a Sunday if I could help it. I lie here dying with only a few weeks left to live so they tell me; and I want to reprimand you sir, for never telling me how to be saved. You never preached the Cross to where I could see it. You never put the Blood out there where I could reach it. Now I'm a dying and I will die in

my sins and I chastise you, sir, for your lack of preaching the true gospel!"

R. G. Lee left that man's hospital room with his head down, feeling berated and guilty as charged. It was now dark outside as he walked down to the banks of the Mississippi River. There he got down on his knees in the mud, getting his white suit pants dirty in the process, while he dipped his hands in the cold muddy river. He knelt there awhile reflecting on what the dying man had told him, it seemed he had been preaching for acceptance and acknowledgement from men rather than for the souls of men. As the moonlight broke over the rippling currents and his arms up to his elbows in the water, right there and then he promised God from that point forward, he would preach the Cross and the Blood, and sin and its remedy, and he changed his message that night. In three weeks time there was a move of grace at his church, and three blocks of downtown Memphis were shaken with revival!

CHAPTER FOUR
THE FIRST MESSAGE OF THE CROSS

"Keeping mercy for thousands, forgiving iniquity and transgression and sin, and that will by no means clear the guilty: visiting the iniquity of the fathers upon the children, and upon the children's children, unto the third and to the fourth generation" (Exodus 34:7).

If we preachers are to preach the Gospel with any authority and power, then it is imperative we understand the message of the Gospel ourselves. The Gospel is not John 3:16. That is part of the Gospel. We must clearly know the real Gospel and its message to sinful man if we are to be Christ's ambassadors. To offer a remedy before a need is felt is casting pearls before swine. In our day of weak evangelism, we beg people to come to Jesus, but they don't feel any need of Him. They are not interested in our Jesus. A man won't go to the doctor unless he discovers he's deathly ill. When a man is sick to the point of death and the doctor has a remedy that will cure him, that man will give that doctor every cent he has to get well and live. But he doesn't need a cure if he doesn't think he's sick.

In the last hundred years pulpits in America have forgotten what the message of the Gospel is. We go around quoting John 3:16 and asking folks to accept Jesus and we think that is preaching the Gospel—but it is an injustice to the Gospel of the Son of God. If you want to be a faithful preacher of the Word then you must go back to square one in the Bible and preach the First Message of the Cross until you are blue in the face and a riot is about to commence in your town. Because if you preach the First Message of the Cross you will have a fight on your hands! That is why Jesus was always ducking His crowd in His earthly ministry; His very first sermon enraged His hearers to where they wanted to forcibly take hold of Him and throw Him headlong over a cliff! We preach nice little messages today that don't disturb anybody—the problem is, they don't save anybody either!

You will have to unplug your brain and swipe it clean of your preconceived ideas of what the Gospel is. I am going to teach you how to preach in this study and you must be willing to accept what I am about to say. When I took Kung Fu, my Sifu asked me if I had ever trained in martial arts before. I said "no". He said, "Good. Then you are an empty cup." In other words, he didn't have to retrain me to unlearn the things I had already ingrained.

If you really want to preach with power and effect for the Kingdom of God then you must learn this first principle of the Gospel message: The First Message of the Cross is GOD WILL PUNISH SIN. Some of you don't believe in a God who would send somebody to Hell. Your god just wouldn't act that way! But the God of the Bible would! The God of the Bible will punish sin and send all rebels to a Devil's hell!

We have so diluted the Gospel message in your day and mine that we have stripped it of all its teeth and power! We have forgotten about the scandal of the Cross! We preachers have gotten out our mop buckets and have cleaned up all the blood and gore around Calvary and made it so pristine that you can sit and have your lunch there! Calvary was a bloody mess! Christ on the Cross was so disfigured from His scourging and beatings that He was almost unrecognizable to His friends! His back was flayed open and its festering wounds oozed to where His back looked like ten pounds of raw hamburger meat!

Christ on the Cross was a scandal! He was stripped naked in public shame and crucified between two common criminals! Yet you want to sing about Calvary like it was just a picnic. We've done away with all the hymns about the Blood; we've preached a bloodless Gospel for years. But that Cross had a bloodstained Savior for sin nailed up there and He was a sight to behold!

The first message of the Cross is GOD WILL PUNISH SIN. We can take a walk through our Bibles and read a running continuous theme: GOD WILL PUNISH SIN.

> *"And God saw that the wickedness of man was great in the earth, and that every imagination of the thoughts of his heart was only evil continually. And it repented the LORD that he had made man on the earth, and it grieved him at his heart. And the LORD said, I will destroy man whom I have created from the face of the earth"* (Genesis 6:5-7).

We see from the lips of the Apostle Peter, that God is a God who will and must punish sin!

"For God spared not the angels that sinned, but cast them down to hell, and delivered them into chains of darkness, to be reserved unto judgment: And spared not the old world, but saved Noah the eight person, a preacher of righteousness, bringing in the flood upon the world of the ungodly: And turning the cities of Sodom and Gomorrah into ashes condemned them with an overthrow, making them an example unto those that after should live ungodly" (2 Peter 2:4-6).

And if you think God has changed His stripes as the God of the Old Testament and the God of the New Testament you are dead wrong!

"For I am the LORD, I change not" (Malachi 3:6).

Some folks think God is more tolerant toward sin these days but they fail to read their Bibles which declare GOD IS A GOD WHO WILL AND MUST PUNISH SIN!

"when the Lord Jesus shall be revealed from heaven with his

mighty angels, In flaming fire taking vengeance on them that know not God, and that obey not the gospel of our Lord Jesus Christ: Who shall be punished with everlasting destruction from the presence of the Lord, and from the glory of his power" (Second Thessalonians 1:6-9).

A big reason why people are uninterested in the Gospel and see no need for Jesus, is they are totally ignorant to the fact that God is a God who will punish sin. The trouble with our society today is that people sleep well at night because they don't believe God will punish sin. They do not believe in that kind of God. Even the majority of church members today do not believe in a God who will punish sin. Their God just wouldn't act that way. But listen, brother preacher, the God of the Bible will because the God of the Bible WILL AND MUST PUNISH SIN! When a church has poor theology, she doesn't act right. The main reason many in our churches today (including ministers) live in Antinomianism is that they do not believe God will punish sin. They are once saved always saved and therefore they can sin all they want to and still go to heaven! So you have a lot of church members who don't let their profession of faith interfere with their daily living because they refuse to believe in a God who would punish sin—especially theirs! We have turned God into a big jolly Santa Claus today who only exists to bless his little darlings. You can quote John 3:16 until you are blue in the face and nobody cares. As you witness to the lost today with an anemic gospel message that has been so watered down it can't save a flea much less a hardened sinner, your witness will fall on deaf ears because they have no interest in Jesus because they refuse to believe God will punish sin. And no one will be interested in what Christ did on the cross until they believe that God will punish sin.

We have forgotten what the message of the gospel is in your day and mine. Our little gospel message speaks only about "an offered Christ" who is standing at the door of your heart knocking and knocking. He is an impotent Jesus who can only stand helplessly there, like an insurance salesman with his hat in this hand, won't you have pity on him and let him in?

Put it down big, plain and straight friend: there is no use to preach the second message of the cross, the forgiveness of sins through

Christ's blood—because there is no use in offering a remedy to people who don't need a remedy! This is why it is critically important to preach the First Message of the Cross: that **GOD IS A GOD WHO WILL PUNISH SIN**. Then once folks realize they are in trouble, in danger, and they need a real remedy for their dirty, filthy, rotten sins, they will flee to Christ for refuge! Go study the sermons of the Puritans, they were masters at preaching the Gospel in its purity and proper order.

This generation of hell bound sinners needs to hear the FIRST message of that bloody cross and that message is **GOD WILL PUNISH SIN.** When those Roman soldiers took hold of Jesus and fastened Him to that tree, as they hammered those rusty nails into the flesh of the Son of God, every stroke of the hammer was an exclamation point crying out: **GOD WILL PUNISH SIN! GOD WILL PUNISH SIN! GOD WILL PUNISH SIN!**

"He that spared not his own Son, but delivered him up for us all, how shall he not with him also freely give us all things" (Romans 8:32).

It is our job as preachers of the Gospel to preach it in its PROPER ORDER. The FIRST MESSAGE OF THE CROSS IS: **GOD WILL**

PUNISH SIN. Then once folks start to believe that then and only then will they feel their need of a Savior for sin—a substitute.

CHAPTER FIVE
THE SECOND MESSAGE OF THE CROSS

"I am crucified with Christ: nevertheless I live; yet not I, but Christ liveth in me; and the life which I now live in the flesh I live by the faith of the Son of God, who loved me, and gave himself for me" (Galatians 2:20)

GOSPEL KNOWLEDGE TEST: describe the gospel. How would you describe the gospel? Tell me what the gospel is.

I don't think many church members today have any comprehension of what the gospel is. They think the gospel is John 3:16.

We must ask ourselves the following question, and how we answer it will reveal much about our view of God and our understanding of the gospel. Answer this question: If the gospel is about salvation and salvation is about being saved, then what are we saved from? [answer: from God's wrath and punishment].

Romans 1:16 clearly demonstrates the gospel message in its intent:

"I am not ashamed of the gospel of Christ, for it is the power of God unto [for] *salvation* [from His wrath and punishment] *to everyone who believes* [in Christ as Savior], *to the Jew first and also to the Greek"*

The Apostle Paul continues his theme of why men need salvation of the Lord:

"For the wrath of God is revealed from heaven against all ungodliness and unrighteousness of men, who hold the truth in unrighteousness" (Romans 1:18).

Few preach the biblical gospel today which is warning to *"flee from the wrath to come."* We tend to view God on human terms and the modern church has turned God into a big jolly Santa Claus who is all love and mercy and who only exists to bless his little darlings. We preach half a gospel today because we refuse to warn men and woman and boys and girls to flee to Christ for salvation from sin and sin's penalty which is damnation in a devil's hell! We have diluted the gospel of all its power, we have extracted all its teeth. Because we don't believe in a God who will and must punish sin. Our God wouldn't send anybody to hell.

The gospel is a message of Good News and invitation to come to Christ for pardon for sin and for salvation from God's wrath and punishment.

The Second Message of the Cross is:

CHRIST THE SUBSTITUTE FOR SIN

Christ died for sinners--

"who loved me, and gave himself for me." [last phrase of Galatians 2:20]

The second message of the Cross is about that substitute who hangs there in my stead. Christ is God's sacrifice and my substitute. I have forgiveness of sins through Christ's blood. Jesus is the cure, the remedy for sin. The second message of the Cross is a lifting up of Christ Jesus as the Savior for sin.

A young Charles Spurgeon was converted to Christ when he heard a simple man preach a simple message of Christ on the Cross as a substitute for sin. His text was from Isaiah,

> *"Look unto Me, and be ye saved, all the ends of the earth, for I am God, and there is none else"* (Isaiah 45:22).

Charles Spurgeon said,

"I looked and saw that bleeding One on the Cross and looked and looked and looked, until I looked my eyes away."

We can present an "offered Christ" after we preach the first message of the cross. People will be hungry, weary, thirsty for relief. The Gospel is for the hungry, the weary, and the thirsty.

We must make sinners thirsty for Christ Jesus by preaching Christ and Him crucified!

"He is despised and rejected of men; a man of sorrows, and acquainted with grief: and we hid as it were our faces from him; he was despised and we esteemed him not. Surely he hath borne our griefs, and carried our sorrows: yet we did esteem him stricken, smitten of God, and afflicted. But he was wounded for our transgressions, he was bruised for our iniquities: the chastisement of our peace was upon him; and with his stripes we are healed. All we like sheep have gone astray; we have turned every one to his own way; and the LORD hath laid on him the iniquity of us all.

He was oppressed, and he was afflicted, yet he opened not his mouth: he is brought as a lamb to the slaughter, and as a sheep before her shearers is dumb, so he openeth not his mouth. He was taken from prison and from judgment: and who shall declare his generation? for he was cut off out of the land of the living: for the transgression of my people was he stricken. And he made his grave with the wicked, and with the rich in his death: because he had done no violence, neither was any deceit in his mouth. Yet is pleased the LORD to bruise him; he hath put him to grief: when thou shalt make his soul an offering for sin, he shall see his seed, and he shall prolong his days, and the pleasure of the LORD shall prosper in his hand. He shall see of the travail of his soul, and shall be satisfied: by his knowledge shall my righteous servant justify many, for he shall bear their iniquities" (Isaiah 53:3-11).

I challenge you friend, to go through the Book of Acts and see how the disciples preached and what message they preached. They would hold up a crucified Christ and point men to a bloodstained Jesus. The Second Message of the Cross: an offered Christ as the sinner's substitute is Good News to sinful man! But it is only good news when it is received and it won't be received until people hear the first message of the cross about a God of justice, who will and must punish sin. But in His mercy He has provided a remedy for sin in the Person of Christ Jesus.

> *"Then the soldiers of the governor took Jesus into the common hall, and gathered unto him the whole band of soldiers. And they stripped him, and put on him a scarlet robe. And when they had plaited a crown of thorns, they put it upon his head, and a reed in his right hand: and they bowed the knee before him, and mocked him, saying, Hail, King of the Jews! And they spit upon him, and took the reed, and smote him on the head. And after that they had mocked him, they took the robe off from him, and put his own raiment*

on him, and led him away to crucify him" (Matthew 27: 27-31).

This is the message of the Gospel: Jesus came down here so we can go up there: He went about doing good, healing the sick, giving sight to the blind, even raising the dead to life. Yet He was taken by cruel hands and led to a place called Calvary where He was crucified. There, He suffered, died, and was buried. On the third day He rose again and appeared unto many; He then ascended back into heaven where He now sits at the right hand of the Father—and He earned that right BY WAY OF A BLOODY CROSS! In John 14:6 Jesus says,

"I am the way, the truth, and the life; no man cometh unto the Father but by me."

Here Jesus answers the three greatest questions of the human heart.

1) How can I be saved? Jesus said, I am the way.
2) How can I be sure? Jesus said, I am the truth.
3) How can I be satisfied? Jesus said, I am the life. And in John 6:35 Jesus declared: "I am the bread of life: he that cometh to

me shall never hunger, and he that believeth on me shall never thirst."

The Gospel is for the hungry, the weary, and the thirsty. Let me ask you friend: Are you hungry for God? Are you sick and tired of your sins? Are you thirsty for Christ. Then come to Him and believe on Him and own Him as your Savior and Lord. The duty required is to come to Christ. And He has a pure gospel promise to all who come: "and him that cometh to me I will in no wise cast out" (v. 37).

The First Message of the Cross is: **GOD WILL PUNISH SIN.**

The Second Message of the Cross: **GOD HAS PROVIDED A REMEDY FOR SIN IN THE PERSON OF CHRIST JESUS!**

CHAPTER SIX
THE FOUR R'S

"When a man starts preaching under the power of the Holy Ghost the great doctrines of the Gospel which are: Ruin, Redemption, Repentance, and Regeneration, then all Hell will begin to break loose!"

E. A. Johnston

We have much activity in our churches today, but very little spiritual activity. We have much teaching in our pulpits today, but very little preaching. At a time when we need preachers instead of teachers this is a serious problem. The great doctrines of the gospel which spurred revival and spiritual awakening in former times lie buried beneath our pulpits today.

Men need to know the badness of their heart or they will rest upon a false bottom of self-righteousness. Men need to be acutely aware of the rottenness of their ruined nature to drive them to God to seek mercy and pardon of sin through the shed blood of Christ Jesus. Men need to be told that they enter this world with a ruined nature and a bent toward sin, and because of their natural state they are under the condemnation of a holy God who hates sin. Men need to be warned to repent and flee from the wrath to come and seek refuge in the Person of Jesus Christ who suffered and died on a bloody Cross for sin. Preachers need to preach the doctrine of Ruin to their people or they will end up with a largely unconverted membership of lost religious people who are ignorant to the holiness of God and the badness of their heart and their desperate danger of dying in their sins. The doctrine of Ruin must be preached so men and women and boys and girls feel their need of a substitute for sin in the Person of Christ Jesus.

It is critically important to the souls of men for a preacher to preach the great doctrines of the Gospel, that men must be informed of the doctrine of Regeneration and man's utter necessity of it, that "Ye must be Born Again" if you desire to see the kingdom of God in heaven. Inform men and women and boys and girls that salvation is not in a decision you make but in the regenerating work of the Spirit of God upon the heart, whereby God takes a heart of stone and makes it a heart of flesh. Because of the watered down, man-centered gospel of our day, multitudes fill our churches as unregenerate church members who have nothing more than an empty religious profession. Their hope of heaven is as empty as a hole in the wall. They have never been born again by God's Spirit. They just reformed some areas in their life and joined the church and were baptized but they have never EXPERIENCED CHANGE.

This is why we have so many wicked deacons, and sin loving church members full of pride and full of self when they should be full of the Holy Ghost.

> *Jesus said, "Except a man be born again he cannot see the kingdom of God"* (John 3:3).

When Jesus was here in His earthly ministry as He passed into towns and villages, all who encountered Him EXPERIENCED CHANGE. We must preach the message: *"Ye must be born again!"* This was the grand theme of the Great Awakening and the main message of George Whitefield and John Wesley who knew full well the emptiness of being lost religious men. Wesley came to America as a missionary to the Indians in Georgia but he was an unconverted minister at the time. He wrote in his diary on the return trip to England, "I came to America to save the Indians, but who will save me?" it was during a bible study on Aldersgate Street in London, while someone was reading the preface to Luther's commentary on Romans, that John Wesley experienced the new birth. He recorded in his diary entry for Wednesday, 24 May 1738:

> "In the evening I went very unwillingly to a society in Aldersgate Street, where one was reading 'Luther's Preface to the Epistle to the Romans'. About a quarter before nine, while he was describing the change which God works in the heart through faith in Christ, I felt my heart strangely warmed. I felt I did trust in Christ, Christ alone, for salvation: and an assurance was given me, that He had taken away my sins, even mine, and saved me from the law of sin and death."

George Whitefield knew that good works could not gain him entrance into heaven; while he was unconverted he fasted, he prayed all night, he denied himself warm clothing and good food, he visited the prisoners and the widows but to no avail—he was just a lost religious man. Until his good friend, Charles

Wesley, loaned him a book by the Scotsman, Henry Scougal, entitled: "The Life of God in the Soul of Man"; that while a young George Whitefield read that little book he realized he lacked the "life of God in his soul" and through this he became born again to where he knew personally, "the life of God in the soul of man" and George Whitefield went out preaching "Ye Must Be Born Again!" and revival followed him on two continents. The doctrine of Regeneration must be proclaimed from our pulpits once again if we have any hope of seeing revival.

The missing doctrine in the modern church today is **Repentance**. The **"Easy Believe Gospel"** has eliminated man's duty of repentance in salvation and has filled Hell with multitudes of church members who never were converted in the first place because they were strangers to repentance.

Preaching the full counsel of God is necessary if we want to see lost souls brought out of darkness and into light. One missing dynamic in our preaching today is the absence of the preaching of the law. George Whitefield and John Wesley both preached the law before grace. In fact, Whitefield said, "A sinner must first be brought to Mt. Sinai before he can be brought to Mt. Zion."

We must warn men that a future judgment awaits all mankind and on That Day, every mother's son will be held up to the unbending law of God in all its strictness and severity. And if you stand there in your own merits you will fail that test for "all have sinned and come short of the glory of God." Your only hope is to stand there in the merits of another, a sin substitute, the Lord Jesus Christ. For God declares that He will "by no means clear the guilty" and that the sentencing of the law will be carried out upon all guilty lawbreakers! The books will be opened and your life reviewed under the intense scrutiny of the One of has eyes of fire! The law is strict and it is severe and it demands perfection! That because of men's danger of dying in their sins and being held accountable to God they need to know God's demand for repentance! Jesus declared,

> *"Except ye repent, ye shall all likewise perish"* (Luke 13:3-5).

Jesus preached repentance:

> *"From that time Jesus began to preach, and to say, Repent: for the*

kingdom of heaven is at hand" (Matthew 4:17).

And we read in Acts the gospel message of the Apostle Paul and the early church:

"Testifying both to the Jews, and also to the Greeks, repentance toward God, and faith toward our Lord Jesus Christ" (Acts 20:21).

As faithful preachers we must warn men about the dangers of damnation and the miseries of Hell and their need of redemption through Christ Jesus. The doctrine of Redemption must be preached in all its demands as well as its benefits. The Gospel of the Son of God has rights and claims on all followers of Him. As blood-bought believers our lives are no longer our own; as Jesus saves not only from the penalty of sin, but from the power of sin. We should live lives of holiness unto him.

If you are a pastor, you must take inventory of your sermons you have preached to your people over the last year. How many sermons did you preach on man's duty of repentance? How many sermons did you preach on man's utter necessity of regeneration? How many sermons did you preach on Ruin, Redemption? How many sermons on Hell have you preached this year already? Men must be confronted with eternity and the God of that eternity. The four R's must be proclaimed!

CHAPTER SEVEN
AWAKEN AND ALARM

"When a man is in a deep lethargy, if you pinch him with

pincers, or prick him with needles, he feels it not. If you

scourge him he cries not, if you threaten him he fears not;

or if you speak to him fair he regards it not. Now, this is

the condition of such that are in a spiritual lethargy: let

the judgments of God be denounced, and let the terrors

of the law be preached, they tremble not; let the flames

of hell-fire flash upon their souls, they regard it not, for

they are sermon-proof, and judgment-proof, and hell-proof."

Thomas Brooks

Preaching is an art that is learned. One must know the mechanics of sermon making: homiletics and hermeneutics are necessary components to sermons and expository preaching is good preaching as it hugs the text and unveils it. However, go study the sermons of the Puritans, or the sermons of the 18th and 19th centuries and see the sparks fly from brimstone falling all about and lightnings flash from Mt. Sinai that is *"altogether on a smoke"* [Exodus 19:18] and see men and women cry out in distress as they led to the very verge of Hell and eternity! And then go compare that to your so-called sermon notes for next Sunday and you'll soon see why your people sit like statues and statuettes in the sanctuary of a cold church that is more like a mortuary than a house of fervent prayer.

Because many churches are in a sad spiritual declension and many church members are in a deep spiritual lethargy, one must preach awakening sermons to rouse them to their danger. We must learn how to preach searching sermons that prick the conscience and disturb those of a spurious conversion.

In Jeremiah chapter twenty three, we find the solution to our need for God declares in verse 29: *"Is not my word like as a fire? saith the LORD: and like a hammer that breaks the rock in pieces?"*

Here the Almighty compares His Word to a fire. what does a fire do? It awakens and alarms. If your family is asleep in your home and during the middle of the night a fire ensues, you will be awakened to smoke alarms and the smell of smoke and it will alarm you. You will gather your loved ones around you as fast as you can and get out of that burning house to safety! We must preach awakening sermons that awaken sinners to their lost condition and alarm backsliders to their danger. Sermons on Hell and the Last Judgement are effective in this regard. Also, our preaching should be as a fire which burns into the conscience bringing conviction of sin. So when God says, His Word is like a fire then we must use it in that capacity!

Also in Jeremiah 23:29 is the other comparison to God's Word—a hammer. What does a hammer do? It busts up things. Our sermons should be crafted so as to bust up all false foundations of an empty religious profession. A good revival sermon should bring the hammer of conviction down; it should pound away at all false refuges and false foundations; sinners must be exposed to the law of God in all its strictness and severity! The great doctrines of the gospel must be hammered home with conviction and authority! Only then can the Spirit of God attend the Word of God and bring transformation to the heart and conscience.

CHAPTER EIGHT
CUTTING MEN DOWN

"Samuel hewed Agag in pieces because King Saul was derelict in his duty to do the same. As preachers, our sermons should cut men asunder bringing conviction of sin."

E. A. Johnston

When one studies the history of revival and reads the sermons that were preached before and during revivals, one will soon discover that the sermons these revival preachers preached were like double edged Claymores used to hew men down, cutting deep into the conscience of sinners and shutting them up to God alone for salvation.

In the Book of Hebrews we read:

"For the word of God is quick, and powerful, and sharper than any two-edged sword, piercing even to the dividing asunder of soul and spirit, and of the joints and marrow, and is a discerner of the thoughts and intents of the heart" (Hebrews 4:12).

I have spent decades reading the sermons that were preached during the Great Awakening and the Second Great Awakening, and they are revealing as to the vital Christianity of the men whom preached them. It is of primary importance to study how God has moved in former times during revivals and spiritual awakenings. We must read the accounts of men whom God has used as revival preachers, so we can learn from their examples and incorporate what they can teach us into our own preaching style to awaken sinners. The following narrative of a sermon preached during the Second Great Awakening out of Genesis chapter nineteen on the destruction of Sodom and it as it was attended with power and influence upon the people who heard it as it was preached from the lips of Charles Finney. This incident is taken Finney's Memoirs:

> "As soon as I had finished the narrative I turned upon them and said, that I understood that they had never had a religious meeting in that place; and that therefore I had a right to take it for granted, and was compelled to take it for granted, that they were an ungodly

people. I pressed that home upon them with more and more energy, with my heart full to bursting.

"I had not spoken to them in this strain of direct application, I should think more than a quarter of an hour, when all at once an awful solemnity seemed to settle down upon them, and a 'some thing' flashed over the congregation,--a kind of shimmering, as if there were some agitation in the atmosphere itself. The congregation began to fall from their seats; and they fell in every direction, and cried for mercy. If I had had a sword in each hand I could not have cut them off their seats as fast as they fell."[1]

Preachers of former times cut men down with the Word of God to bring revival and the salvation of souls! Often, the preaching during times of revival would transform the moral life of an entire community. The evangelist Sam Jones was mighty hewing men down with the sword of the Lord and his ministry often

---

[1] Charles Finney, "Finney's Memoirs", (Grand Rapids: Academie Books, 1989). pp 101-102.

reformed the spiritual life of a town. We see this from the following:

"Reform is a city in Pickens County Alabama and is located halfway between Columbus, Mississippi and Tuscaloosa on Route 82. The city records state it was named Reform after a visit by an evangelist.

"Reform, Alabama was named after the evangelist Sam Jones conducted revival meetings there. Sam Jones came into town and preached for eight weeks and when he left town there was nobody in the jail, the theaters were closed, nobody played cards, and the liquor stores were run out of business. There wasn't anything questionable left. And when men would curse in the streets they would lower their voices, so nobody could hear them."[2]

---

[2] E. A. Johnston, "Sam Jones A New Biography", (Gainesville: The Old Paths Publications, 2023), Back cover.

CHAPTER NINE
THE GOSPEL MUST BE PREACHED IN ITS PURITY AND PROPER ORDER

"Modern evangelism offers Jesus like a free stick of chewing gum, and people accept our 'little Jesus' and chew on him for a while—until the flavor goes out of their religion."

E. A. Johnston

The modern evangelist portrays a impotent Jesus standing helplessly at the door of your heart, like an insurance salesman with his hat in his hand. Won't you let him in? And if we do let him into our heart, we can do it when we are good and ready. And we preachers have so diluted the gospel of anything offensive to make it more palatable to modern man. Preachers today have gotten out their mop buckets and cleaned up all the blood and gore around Calvary to make it so pristine you can sit and have your lunch there.

The great failure of evangelism in our day is the sad reality that we have taken salvation out of the hands of God and placed it in the hands of men; and we have shrunken God down to man's size and placed Him on our level. We removed anything objectionable from our churches so not to offend anybody—we quit singing all the old hymns about the Blood, we quit preaching about the Blood, and we ceased offering a bloodstained Savior for sin. In its place, we offer an agreeable Jesus who came to earth to make men's life a little better while they are here and to give them bliss for eternity. God is no longer the God of the Old Testament full of smoke and judgment—the God we preach is a Santa Claus God who is here to bless and favor his little darlings and he is a being who is now more tolerant toward sin. Meanwhile, the unconverted fill our church membership and Hell fills by the hour with the Hellbound who have never, ever, heard the real gospel in their entire life.

The real Gospel is a God-centered Gospel about a thrice holy God who saves sinners for His own glory; and if you want Him you must shut yourself up entirely to Him because He sent His only begotten Son to suffer and die on a scandalous Cross suffering the shame and pain of Calvary; and the only way to get your sins pardoned is you must come to this Jesus and surrender to Him and throw down your shotgun of rebellion at His nail-pierced feet and believe on Him and own Him as your Savior and Lord. Then you must take up your cross and follow him in a life of discipleship, whereby self is dethroned and another is enthroned there—the Lord Jesus Christ!

The Gospel declares Christ died for sinners, do you feel your need for a Savior from sin? The gospel is for the hungry, the weary, and the thirsty. Let me ask you a question friend: Are you hungry for God? Are you sick and tired of your sins? Are you thirsty for Christ? Then come to Him and believe on Him. Jesus declares:

> *"If any man thirst, let him come unto me and drink. He that believeth on me, as the Scripture hath said, out of his belly shall flow rivers of living water"* (John 7:37-38).

We must learn how to preach an exalted God and a bloodstained Christ who died for sin. And that men everywhere must repent because God demands repentance for salvation. And if you want to see the kingdom of God then you must be Born Again, whereby the Spirit of God wrought a work of grace upon the heart in the supernatural act of regeneration. You must be born from above and washed in the Blood!

RUIN

Your nature is cursed. Old Adam is under a curse. I was born in the likeness of my father, and he was born in the likeness of his father, all the way to Adam.

> *"Wherefore, as by one man sin entered into the world, and death by sin; and so death passed upon all men, for that all have sinned"* (Romans 5:12).

We each enter this world with a ruined nature and bent toward sin. Our natural condition is under the condemnation of God. Our only hope is Jesus.

We must preach searching sermons on the sinfulness of sin. On the depravity and wickedness of the human heart.

> *"The heart is deceitful above all things, and desperatey wicked: who can know it"* (Jeremiah 17:9)?

Men must be shown their own heart in all its vivid colors so they won't rest on a false foundation of self-righteousness.

REDEMPTION

Blood redemption is a topic we all should be familiar with. From the Old Testament priests who would kill an unblemished lamb and offer it as a sacrifice as a sin offering for the people. So too, Christ is our substitute for sin, our sin offering. There is no redemption without blood.

In the ancient city of Ephesus is an agora, the reconstructed ruins of which I visited. An agora in ancient times was a marketplace where items were bought and sold, kind of like a shopping mall today. A Greek word for redemption is "agorazzo" which has that word "agora" in it. "agorazzo" means that Christ entered the marketplace of sin and purchased me by His death and with His blood. The little Greek preposition, "ek" placed in front of the word "agorazzo" –"ek-agorazzo" means that Christ entered the marketplace of sin and **brought me up and out of it**. Christ died to save me from the penalty of sin as well as the power of sin!

REPENTANCE

The only-believe gospel is a heretical gospel that has damned its multitudes. The only-believe gospel holds the position that all you have to do to be saved is believe; repentance is not a necessary component of salvation. But one has to use razor blade theology to come to that conclusion because the whole of the gospel is a gospel of repentance. Jesus declared:

> *"I tell you, Nay; but, except ye repent, ye shall all likewise perish"* (Luke 13:3),

and that means YOU, even if you are the chairman of the deacons!)

The gospel is repent! Jesus' disciples preached repentance. "And they went out and preached that men should repent" (Mark 6:12). Jesus began His earthly ministry by preaching repentance:

> *"Now after that John was put in prison, Jesus came into Galilee, preaching the gospel of the kingdom of God, and saying, "The time is fulfilled, and the kingdom of God is at hand, repent ye, and believe the gospel"* (Mark 1:14-15).

After His resurrection from the dead, Jesus commanded:

> *"Repentance and remission of sins should be preached in his name"* (Luke 24:47).

The Apostle Paul preached the doctrine of repentance as well as part of the gospel:

"Testifying both to the Jews, and also to the Greeks, repentance toward God, and faith toward our Lord Jesus Christ" (Acts 20:21).

If you are a preacher and you have never preached repentance then you have never repented yourself.

REGENERATION

George Whitefield brought revival to two continents preaching one main message: "Ye must be born again!" A young George Whitefield knew what it was like to try to earn his way into heaven. As a member of John Wesley's Holy Club at Oxford, he fasted, prayed entire nights, gave alms, visited the widow and prisoner, he denied himself warm clothing in inclement weather but he was yet an unconverted religious man. Until one day his good friend, Charles Wesley loaned him a book written by the Scotsman, Henry Scougal, entitled, "The Life of God in the Soul of Man" and while reading that book Whitefield realized he needed to be born again by the regenerating work of the Holy Spirit so he could know personally, the life of God in the soul of man!

Many revivals have begun when faithful ministers began to preach searching sermons on the doctrine of regeneration. This happened in Cambuslang, Scotland in 1742 when William M'Culloch began a series of sermons on regeneration which caused quite a commotion in his church and grew into the Cambuslang Revival, where 50,000 people gathered on the Preaching Brae's below the church to hear fourteen ministers preach night and day on the great doctrines of the gospel.

Jesus taught about the utter necessity of a work of grace upon the heart through the supernatural act of regeneration by God's Spirit. "Jesus answered and said unto him, except a man be born again, he cannot see the kingdom of God" (John 3:3).

In a day of sad spiritual declension in our churches, we must ask ourselves a burning question: "Are men converted by a decision they make? Or by the regenerating work of the Holy Spirit?" Preaching on man's need of regeneration will spark a revival more than many other topics. Many in our churches today rest upon the rotten foundation of an empty religious profession. Therefore, it is critically important to preach sermons on the doctrine of regeneration.

CHAPTER TEN
THE SPIRIT'S ANOINTING

"Men like Jonathan Edwards and George Whitefield, D. L. Moody and Sam Jones, were mightily used of God in times of revival because they were men full of the Holy Ghost."

E. A. Johnston

I am deeply moved when I read the story of the Puritan, Thomas Goodwin, who after hearing Rogers of Dedham preach, hung "a quarter of an hour upon the neck of his horse weeping, before he had power to mount."

Does your preaching do that?

During seasons of revival and awakening, there is a such a demonstration of the Spirit that attends the word preached that many come to Christ in one sermon.

"Five hundred people traced their conversion to one sermon preached by John Livingstone at Kirk O' Shotts in 1630—and believers overwhelmed with the force of the truth."[3]

The missing element in today's preaching is anointing of the Spirit. D. L. Moody's entire ministry was changed when he realized his need for the Spirit's anointing. The mandate is clear:

"But ye shall receive power, after that the Holy Ghost is come upon you: and ye shall be witnesses unto me both in Jerusalem, and in all Judea, and in Samaria, and unto the uttermost part of the earth" (Acts 1:8).

"When one studies historical revival certain truths emerge as they are unearthed in accentuating the common denominator in revival. It is always the manifest presence of God by His Spirit that brings awakening, conviction, and conversions.

"It is no coincidence that the three most used American evan-

---

[3] Iain Murray, "Puritan Papers, Volume One", (Phillipsburg: P&R Publishing, 2000), pp 3-4.

gelists of the 19th century each shared a common experience—an enduement of Holy Ghost power for service. It happened to Charles Finney, D. L. Moody, and Sam Jones. This was the secret to their power. And this anointing occurred to each of them BEFORE they were thrust onto a national stage of great usefulness.

"It came to Dwight Lyman Moody in 1871, before he was greatly used of God in revival throughout Great Britain. It happened to Charles Grandison Finney before he was used of God in revivals during the Second Great Awakening. And it happened to Samuel Porter Jones before he was thrust into the national spotlight and so powerfully used in revivals throughout the whole of America."[4]

The men I have known who had power in the pulpit as preachers were each men filled with an anointing of the Spirit.

---

[4] E. A. Johnston, "Sam Jones A New Biography", (Gainesville: The Old Paths Publications, 2023), pp 185-186.

My homiletical mentor, Dr. Stephen F. Olford illustrated this clearly one day in his office as he sat with me. He entered his office and slumped down into a chair beside me. He began to apologize to me: "Pardon me brother, pardon me. I need a few minutes to regather myself. I just preached and virtue has left me!" immediately, as Dr. Olford said that, I thought of Jesus in a crowded street and the woman with the issue of blood touched the hem of his garment we see from the text:

"And Jesus immediately knowing in himself that virtue had gone out of him, turned him about in the press, and said, Who touched my clothes?" (Mark 5:25-34).

Let me ask you brother preacher. When you preach does virtue leave you?

There is a cost to get this anointing. Not a monetary cost but a physical one. Anything worthwhile has a sacrifice associated with it whether its higher education or learning a trade or craft. What costs counts and what counts costs.

Dr. Stephen Olford wrote in the flyleaf of my evangelist friend, David Ford's Bible the following inscription:

The Anointing of the Spirit

Conditions:

1) Holiness
2) Yieldedness
3) Prayerfulness

One preacher, who understood this principle of the anointing of the Spirit was Dr. Martyn Lloyd-Jones, who for almost thirty years was the minister of Westminster Chapel in London. He was a master at expository preaching, often taking an entire month to expand a chapter of the bible verse by verse. It was said of him that while he was preaching it was not uncommon for his hearers to be brought to the very verge of eternity as if the very spiritual atmosphere of the church had been suddenly altered. Lloyd-Jones understood this deeper dimension of preaching with unction and authority. Dr. Martyn Lloyd-Jones understood the great need for a baptism of the Holy Ghost.

"Has there been a great call to prayer and fasting and humiliation? A crying out to God to have mercy, and to baptize us afresh with the Holy Ghost?"[5]

Dr. Lloyd-Jones believed that not only was there a deep need to be filled with the Spirit for ministry, he recognized the reality of the manifest presence of the Spirit in seasons of revival. We see from the following remarks:

> "What happens to the Church, first of all, when God hears the cry and begins to answer? The first thing really is that the Church becomes conscious of a presence and a power in her midst…this sense of God, the presence and the presidency of the Holy Ghost…God has become a reality to them, God has come down, as it were, into their midst. The meeting is taken out of the hands of whoever who may have been in charge, and the Holy Ghost begins to preside, and to take charge, and everybody is

---

[5] Martyn Lloyd-Jones, "Revival", (Wheaton: Crossway Books, 1987), p 202.

aware of his presence, and of his glory, and of his power."[6]

I cannot emphasize this element in preaching enough. This attending of the Holy Spirit when we preach. It seems to be the missing element in our churches today. If we desire power in the pulpit, we must seek this unction from on High!

[6] Ibid, pp 203-204.

CHAPTER ELEVEN
THE FINAL JUDGMENT

"The Holy Spirit moved mightily amongst us. The listeners felt as though they were at the judgment stand, a total of 1,363 repented and 80 people dedicated their lives to become preachers."
John Sung,
Singapore, 1935.

It is the duty of all preachers to warn their hearers about a future judgment that awaits all mankind. Preaching on the Last Judgment is a very useful means to arouse concern over one's soul and eternal destiny. If we fail to preach on the Final Judgment, then we fail as ambassadors to Christ.

I preached at a church on the Last Judgment and saw a powerful revival commence among the people of God. We must prepare sermons to preach on the Great White Throne Judgement that awaits all mankind. When men and women and boys and girls are confronted with eternity and the God of that eternity then things will begin to pop! The church where I preached on the Final Judgement was greatly stirred by the Spirit of

God. When I finished preaching and sat down, a young man came running down the aisle hollering, "I just got saved! I just got saved! I really just got saved!" The music minister afterwards told me that while I was preaching on the Last Judgment, he saw Jesus sitting on His throne. It is of immense importance that we become deeply familiar with the following striking passage of Scripture from the Book of Revelation, in chapter twenty, in verses 11-15. I strongly recommend committing this entire passage to memory, so you can preach it from memory.

"And I saw a great white throne, and him that sat on it, from whose face the earth and the heaven fled away; and there was found no place for them.

"And I saw the dead, small and great, stand before God; and the books were opened: and another book was opened, which is the book of life: and the dead were judged out of those things which were written in the books, according to their works.

"And the sea gave up the dead which were in it; and death

and hell delivered up the dead which were in them: and they were judged every man according to their works.

"And death and hell were cast into the lake of fire. This is the second death.

"And whosoever was not found written in the book of life was cast into the lake of fire."

As you preach this message in the power of the Holy Ghost, your hearers will be brought to the very verge of eternity to be faced with the God of that eternity. We see that the throne mentioned is the Great White Throne. It is great because of who sits there; it is white because God is holy. It is a throne because "all things" are committed into those nail-pierced hands of the one who sits there. The mention of earth and heaven fleeing away from His presence is a vivid picture of the final dissolution of earth and all things in it. Nothing material holds any worth in eternity—it is as dust in the wind.

There is a vast crowd assembled there on That Day. John Wesley called it The Grand Assize, or great judgment. Every mother's son from every age and epoch of history is standing there before that great white throne and the One on the throne has all the time in the world to review each person's life one-by-one as they pass before His bench of justice. The books are opened and every one there is judged out of those things which are written in the books. There before the Judge of all the earth sits your life story, your biography opened before Him. Every line on every page represents every moment and every day you ever lived. All your thoughts are written there, all your deeds—whether good or bad, all you words that you spoke—those spoken in the heat of anger as well as those spoken by lies. And behind every action, thought and word, is the motive representing it. And as the books are opened on your life the Judge with eyes of fire reviews every single jot and tittle beneath His intense scrutiny!

It is a heavenly court room scene, if I may so speak, where the baliffs are the angels in charge of the books and record of each life; the devil is the prosecuting attorney the accuser of the brethren. As in a courtroom, cases will be reviewed, evidence presented, the sentencing of the law carried out upon all guilty lawbreakers. And every person standing there before that Throne of Justice, the small and the great, the rich and the poor, the famous and the unknown, each one will be held up against the strictness and severity of God's unbending law, and all will be found guilty and fail that test if they stand there in their own merits, for, "all have sinned and come short of the glory of God." You must stand there in the merits of another—a sin substitute—the Lord Jesus Christ.

They call my name and I am escorted by a strong angel to the Great White Throne and that eternal platform where all eyes can see me standing there before the Judge and shall not the Judge of all the earth do right? As I stand there my thoughts race back to a story I heard years ago. There was a man traveling though the city of St. Louis and it was a Sunday and he was a Christian, so he parked his car at a downtown church and went inside to worship. Once in there, he realized he was the only white person in an all black church, so he took his seat on the back row. Up on the platform was the elderly pastor who was giving his subject for that particular morning and his subject was heaven. He began by saying, "Some folks call heaven paradise, other folks call it Abraham's bosom. I like to think of heaven this a'way. Here is Jesus, just returned from His earthly ministry and He's standing at those pearly gates and old Gabriel greets Him. "Hello Jesus! Sure is good to see you Jesus! We sure missed You up here Jesus. Welcome home Jesus!—but wait! Whose that with you? Is that that thief from the cross? Oh no Sir, we can't have no thieves up here! He's not welcome here!" Jesus replied, "Never you mind Gabriel, never you mind," and just then Jesus placed His arm around the thief and declared, "He's with Me!"

That is the story I am thinking about as I stand before that Great White Throne and face that Judge sitting there. He is holy and I am a sinner. And as the strictness and severity of His law is held up against the works of my life I begin to tremble, because I know I am not perfect. I can hear laughter, a taunting mocking laughter from the prosecuting attorney—the devil himself. He knows he's got me dead to rights! I am guilty! But just then the Judge rises from His throne, and He walks behind me as my Advocate, my defense attorney, and He wraps His arm around me and declares in a loud voice to that vast crowd assembled there: "HE'S WITH ME!" And the angels start singing, and bells start ringing and I hear shouts of praise. And I see my friends and loved ones standing there to greet me and welcome into glory!

I highly recommend that you read the sermons of Thomas Brooks, Joseph Alliene, Solomon Stoddard, and Jonathan Edwards to get a sense of how the preach the law before grace. George Whitefield used to say,

> "A sinner must be brought to Mt. Sinai before he can come to Mt. Zion."

It is vastly important, fellow preacher, to get your own individual sermon on the Last Judgment and fill it with some good illustrations then preach it frequently and you will be surprised by the results!

CHAPTER TWELVE
PREACHING TO THE CONSCIENCE

"Asahel Nettleton, was the primary leader of the time period known as The Second Great Awakening. His sermons were not like a shotgun that hit you all over, they were more like a sharpshooter rifle aimed at the very conscience of men. When preaching the evening service in a church in Pittsfield, MA in 1828 out of Genesis 19, it was said his descriptions of the burning of Sodom was so descriptive and unsettling that 'it turned the heads of the congregation toward the windows to witness the conflagration.'"

E. A. Johnston

There is a common denominator in revival preaching that can be found in the sermons of John Wesley, George Whitefield, Jonathan Edwards, Charles Finney and other men used during times of revival and spiritual awakening and it is prominent in the sermons of the Puritans; such as Solomon Stoddard, Thomas Brooks, Thomas Shepherd, and

Joseph Alliene. This common denominator is the spark and fire of all good revival preaching and it is when a sermon is not preached to the head but to the consciences of men. Sound revival preaching will aim for the conscience to alarm it, awaken it, disturb it, and make the hearer flee to Christ for refuge from sin. It will be the kind of preaching that has long term effects upon a people or town by pushing back the darkness in a community.

Observe the following comments of an eyewitness to Sam Jones coming to his town of Thomson, Georgia in 1877:

> "In the good year of 1877, Sam Jones lit down in this veritable town of Thomson, and began to go for the Devil and his angels in a manner which was entirely new to said Devil; also new to said angels.

> "Someone happened to remark in my hearing that there was a little preacher up at the Methodist church who was knocking the crockery around in a lively style, and who was dusting the jackets of the amen corner brethren, in a way which brought the double grunts out of those fuzzy fossils.

"I was not ravenously fond of sermons. I did not yawn the day I went to hear Sam Jones. There he was, clad in a little black, jump-tail coat, and looking very little like the regulation preacher. He was not in the pulpit. He was right next to his crowd, standing within the railings, and almost in touch of the victims. His head was down, as if he was holding onto his chain of thought by the teeth, but his right hand was going energetically up and down, with all the grace of a pump-handle. And, how he did hammer the brethren. How he did peel the amen corner. How he did smash their solemn self-conceit, their profound self-satisfaction, their peaceful partnership with the Almighty, their placid conviction that they were the trustees of the New Jerusalem! After a while, with solemn irresistible force he called on these brethren to rise in public, confess their shortcomings, and kneel for Divine grace.

"And they knelt. With groans, and sobs, and tears, these old bellweathers of the flock fell on their knees and cried aloud in their distress. Then what? He turned his guns upon us sinners. He raked us fore and aft. He gave us grape and canister and all the rest. He abused us and ridiculed us; he stormed at us and laughed at us; he called us flop-eared hounds, beer kegs, and whisky soaks. He plainly said that we were all hypocrites and liars, and he intimated somewhat broadly that most of us would steal.

"Oh, we had a time of it, I assure you. For six weeks the farms and the stores were neglected, and Jones! Jones! Jones! was the whole thing.

"And the pleasant feature of the entire display of human nature was the marked manner in which the 'amen-corner brethren' enjoyed his flaying of us sinners.

"Well, the meeting wound up, the community settled back into its old ways—but it has never been the same community since. Gambling disappeared, loud profanity on the streets was heard no more, and the barrooms were run out of the county."[7]

Mordecai Ham was another evangelist who preached to the conscience of men and saw the entire moral life of communities altered. The following description of him is typical of his preaching and the impact it had on the towns he preached in:

"When evangelist Ham preached, mockers were converted, families were restored, bars were closed, laws were changed, churches were filled to overflowing (one even advertised in the paper that no more new converts should attend as there was not room for them), hundreds were called to preach, and crooked politicians either repented or feared the consequences. When some resisted God's work, God withdrew

---

[7] E. A. Johnston, "Sam Jones A New Biography", (Gainesville: The Old Paths Publications, 2023), pp 66-68.

His grace in answer to Ham's prayers and God's judgment fell."[8]

Jonathan Edwards was a preacher who preached directly to the consciences of men. His sermon, "Sinners In The Hands Of An Angry God" caused such a commotion a revival broke out in the Enfield Meeting House, on July 8th, 1741. Stephen Williams was an eyewitness and wrote in his diary:

> "We went over to Enfield—where we met dear Mr. E of NH who preached a most awakening sermon from these words—Deut. 32-35 and before sermon was done—there was a great moaning and crying out through ye whole House—What Shall I do to be saved—oh I am going to Hell—Oh what shall I do for Christ &c. So ye minister was obliged to desist—ye shrieks and cries were piercing and Amazing—"[9]

---

[8] Edward E. Ham, "50 Years On The Battle Front With Christ: A Biography of Mordecai Ham", (Shelbyville: Bible & Literature Missionary Foundation, 2005), p 2.

[9] Oliver Means, "A Sketch of the Strict Congregational Church of Enfield, Conn.," (Hartford: 1899), p 192

What we have mainly in our pulpits today are either entertainers who want to make you laugh and have a good time or teachers who want to feed your mind with essays to be considered. What we need are men who are willing to fight the Devil tooth and nail and storm the gates of Hell by preaching searching sermons aimed at the consciences of men! Instead of having our audiences laughing in the aisles we need them in distress and crying out, "What must I do to be saved?"

Only a serious ministry burdened with the souls of men will invest the time to produce messages that will arouse men and women out of their spiritual slumber and show them their perilous position outside of Christ's Blood. There is a cost to get the Sprit's anointing for preaching but whatever the cost is—it is well worth it because eternity hangs in the balance.

CHAPTER THIRTEEN
GETTING MEN LOST

"Have you ever been lost? Are you a lost sinner? How do you know you are saved if you've never been lost?"

E. A. Johnston

Jesus made a startling statement concerning who He saves:

"For the Son of man is come to seek and to save that which was lost" (Luke 19:10).

If Jesus said it, why do we ignore it when we preach the Gospel? One of the greatest failures of modern evangelism is that we offer folks our little Jesus before they feel any need of Him. Old Time preachers like Sam Jones and Mordecai Ham used to preach hard to get men lost before they could get them saved. Both of these evangelists would go to work on their hearers with the express purpose to "strip the bark off of them" so the Holy Spirit could reveal to them that they were resting upon a rotten foundation of an empty religious profession—and they would get men lost. Sam Jones and Mordecai Ham didn't offer folks a remedy for sin before they made sure their hearers felt their need of a remedy for sin—to do otherwise was to cast pearls before swine.

I have a sermon that I have preached through the years and it encapsulates this notion of getting men lost. Here now, is that sermon:

SAVED OR LOST?

I want to share a story with you friend where a young man's life was changed. Two college boys were roommates, one was a Christian and the other was not. One night the Christian boy asked his friend if he would join him in attending a tent revival meeting being held in that college town by a itinerant evangelist. It was only two blocks away from their dormitory and they could walk there, it was a pleasant night. The roommate who wasn't a Christian only agreed to go because it would be an excuse not to study his economics book.

So they walked across campus to this outdoor meeting. As they drew closer they could hear the preacher, he had a thick Southern accent, and this appealed to the non-Christian who was from the South himself. He had forgotten what a Southerner sounded like among so many Mid-Western folk.

The evangelist was an old man and his voice trembled when he spoke as he told of a bleeding Savior hanging on a bloodstained cross for sin. The preacher went into great detail as he described what a crucifixion entailed. He used the most graphic terms with all the ramifications of death on a cross: the awful suffering, the terrible dehydration, the loss of blood which made one nauseous, the weakness and painful contractions of the muscles in the legs to support the battered body that had been whipped viciously by a cruel Roman soldier holding a scourge of broken glass and nails at the end of a hand rope. The old preacher described in the most sickening terms the reality of the beating of Christ: how the backside of Jesus was so cut and lacerated and torn up that it looked like ten pounds of raw hamburger meat out in the sun with flies on it! The thought of it made the unsaved boy squeamish in his stomach and weak in the knees. But the preacher kept on with his graphic descriptions of the battered body of that Christ on that Cross.

Then the preacher made a statement that the unsaved boy felt he was directing exactly toward him: he said, "Jesus can save even you. Jesus can save even you" (and the old man made eye contact with the college boy as he said it). The preacher went on, "I'll say it again: Jesus can save EVEN YOU. Why, He saved one of the thieves right next to him when that condemned criminal trusted Christ to save him." "But", the evangelist pointed out, "that thief had to own up to his own guilt in being a lost sinner in need of a Savior." Then the evangelist said, "Jesus is the Pearl of great price worth selling all for so He may be gained. But you must feel your need of Him. Only a sin sick individual needs a remedy for sin. Jesus didn't come to call the righteous but sinners to repentance."

Then the old man closed his message with the following request: he said, "Friends, all I want you to do tonight is to go home quietly, thinking about what you have heard tonight concerning the love of the Father who gave His only begotten Son to hang naked on a bloody Cross for sinners. Are you a sinner? Jesus said, *'The Son of man is come to seek and to save that which was lost.'* Are you a lost sinner? Do me a favor friends—all I ask of you is to go home tonight and take a piece of paper or an index card and write one word on it: write the word in capital letters SAVED or LOST. If you're saved and you know it, then write

SAVED and go to bed in perfect peace knowing if you died in the night, you'd wake up in the arms of Jesus! On the other hand, if you are a lost sinner, I want you to have the courage to write the word LOST and I want you to think about where you would end up if you died tonight outside the saving Blood of Christ Jesus; and the terrible torments you would endure for all eternity in a devil's Hell! Then the Southern preacher closed the meeting without even giving an invitation. Which shocked everyone. The old man just closed his Bible, wiped a tear from his cheek, and before he left the platform he called out in voice trembling with emotion: "Dear lost friend, no matter what terrible thing you've done in life—Jesus can save even YOU!" The old man was so worn out he could barely make it off the platform on his shaky legs.

The two roommates walked back to their dormitory in complete silence. Each was afraid to speak to the other. Back at the dorm room they climbed into each of their own beds. The Christian read his Bible awhile and before turning out the light on his bed stand, he wrote on a piece of paper the word SAVED and then turned out the light and went to sleep.

The other boy couldn't sleep for a million dollars—he was so torn up inside with guilt and he felt horrible. He knew he couldn't write the word SAVED on his piece of paper cause he knew he wasn't saved. But he could NOT bring himself to write the word LOST. The boy was torn up with guilt because he had done something terrible nobody knew about. There was an old lady who lived next door to his parent's farm and he hated her. She had squealed to his parents about how he stole her sack of groceries that were on her porch one day. And he had gotten a whipping from his strict father who seemed to be always whipping his rebellious son. And the boy never forgave that old woman for telling on him. And she was an old widow who lived alone and her only companion was her fat Calico cat that stayed in her bony lap. One day, while she was out, the boy took that cat behind his barn and strangled it until it was dead, then he buried it in the yonder woods. And it wasn't long that he regretted killing that cat, for the cries of that old lady kept him up that night when her cat never came back home. And for the last twelve years he had lived with the guilt of that crime.

As the boy lay in bed, those words of the old preacher rang in his ears: "Dear sinner friend, Jesus can save even you." And he also recalled the preacher quoting Jesus who said: *"For the Son of man has come to seek and to save that which was lost."* Finally, at about 2am, the boy got out of bed and grabbed the piece of paper and wrote the word LOST. Then he dropped to his knees and admitted to a holy God that he was a big sinner who was lost and on his way to hell; and he needed to be saved. He asked God to forgive him for killing that old lady's cat and then he thought of a lot more sins he needed to confess. Finally, a ray of light came into his soul and with joy in his heart he grabbed that piece of paper and crossed out the word LOST and, in its place, wrote in big letters SAVED with an exclamation point!

I like that story because it's so true. Jesus can save even you friend. As preachers of the gospel we need to get men lost before they can be saved. Let's never forget that as we proclaim the Good News to a lost and perishing generation!

CHAPTER FOURTEEN
PREACHING AND PRAYER

"Revd William E. Schubert often went into a fasting prayer and cries of worship could often be heard from upstairs. 'O God! Isn't it time to revive the church at Nanchang? If not now, when? There's no point for me to stay here if you don't' show any mercy! I might as well go back to my country.' His earnest prayers touched the very depths of my heart indeed."

John Sung

When one studies the history of preaching and revival it is often discovered that the greatest preachers were the greatest prayers. Charles Finney would not think of entering a pulpit unless he had spent the previous day or evening in desperate prayer. John Wesley and George Whitefield spent entire nights in prayer and fasting before the revival occurred in England. John Sung's daughter Levi said of him, "Four or five hours at a time were not too long to pray for him." And John Sung shook China for God in powerful revivals because he first and foremost a man of prayer.

My homiletical mentor, Dr. Stephen F. Olford was a diminutive man out of the pulpit but once he stood behind a pulpit he appeared as a giant! He preached with great power and authority. But Stephen Olford knew he was only as tall in the pulpit as he was long on his knees in prayer. A book I highly commend to you E. M. Bounds book, entitled *"Preacher and Prayer."* It is a rich storehouse of gems on the subject of preaching and prayer.

I want to bring this thought home to you about preaching and prayer by an incident I witnessed many years ago. A friend of mine preached at a church in the South and before he preached his first message at that church, the people gathered in the sanctuary to pray for the preacher and the effect of the sermon. For forty-five minutes these sincere believers prayed fervently for my evangelist friend. And when he got up to preach there was such a power upon him, that I sat at the back of the room weeping. The next evening, there was no one there early to pray and my friend entered the pulpit and preached a mediocre message that fell flat as a pancake. Why the difference? I believe it was the lack of fervent prayer that attended his first message but was absent from his second message.

When a sermon is bathed in fervent prayer it has an energy, a life, a force from above—an unction. We get a sense of this from the words of E. M. Bounds:

"This unction comes to the preacher not in the study but in the closet. It is heaven's distillation in answer to prayer. It is the sweetest exhalation of the Holy Spirit. It impregnates, suffuses, softens, percolates, cuts, and soothes. It carries the Word like dynamite, like salt, like sugar; makes the Word a soother an arraigner, a revealer, a searcher; makes the hearer a culprit or a saint, makes him weep like a child and live like a giant; opens his heart and his purse as gently, yet as strongly as the spring opens the leaves. This unction is not the gift of genius. It is not found in the halls of learning. No eloquence can woo it. No industry can win it. No prelatical hands can confer it. It is the gift of God—the signet set to his own messengers."[10]

My homiletical mentor, Dr. Stephen F. Olford saw revival at Wheaton College in the 1960's when he was preaching there at chapel. One young man wrote in his journal the effects of the preaching had altered his life—the young man was Jim Elliot, the missionary martyr. Decades later, his widow Elizabeth Elliot visited Stephen Olford and showed him the journal entry made by Jim Elliot that day. As Dr. Olford related that story to me, he added, "it all began when I was out of bed all night in prayer before I preached the next day."

I've heard Dr. Olford comment to a congregation: "I had a message prepared for today, but at 2am this morning, the Lord told me that wasn't the message! And I had put a lot of time in it as well! But it will keep." Dr. Stephen F. Olford would spend time out of bed during the evening hours praying over his message he was to preach that next day. Charles Finney would often spend an entire afternoon in the woods, on his knees crying out to God in prayer over the people he was to

---

[10] E. M. Bounds, "Preacher And Prayer", (Asheville: Revival Literature, 2013), p 69.

preach to that evening. We must bathe our preaching in prayer for it to have any power.

There is a story about the great British preacher, Charles Spurgeon that resonates with this matter of preaching and prayer. A young seminary graduate visited Charles Spurgeon at the Metropolitan Tabernacle, an hour before the Sunday morning service. Spurgeon asked the young man if he would like to see the engine of the church. The young man said he would. Spurgeon led him down a corridor of stairs to the basement to where two double doors stood closed. The young man thought the pastor had taken him to the church's boiler room. But upon opening the double doors, the young man saw 300 deacons on their knees bowed in prayer. Spurgeon smiled and announced: "See here my engine of the church!" The entire time Charles Spurgeon preached to his vast crowd the basement was full of hundreds of sincere men praying to God for power to fall!

Unfortunately, in our churches today many have replaced the weekly prayer meeting with divorce recovery classes or Zumba dance, or Yoga lessons! If the prayer meeting is the engine of the church, then that explains why so many churches are out of gas!

CHAPTER FIFTEEN
USING ILLUSTRATIONS

"The proper use of illustrations in preaching can strengthen and enlighten a text. Jesus used illustrations from agriculture and farming for his hearers were sheepherders and farmers. The best preachers use illustrations when they preach and often the use of illustrations is what makes them great preachers. George Whitefield's mastery over an audience was in his dramatic illustrations and the drama he used to make them come alive."

E. A. Johnston

George Whitefield, the great British evangelist used illustrations when he preached to bring excitement and attention to his sermons. On one such occasion while preaching to royalty in the parlor of a London mansion, he was describing the poor plight of the lost sinner by comparing him to a blind beggar walking near a dangerous precipice. Here was the poor blind beggar and his little dog beside him while he leaned on his cane for balance and direction, and as Whitefield enlarged his text and heightened the danger of the scene we read from the following:

"The anecdote of Lord Chesterfield, I believe, is not disputed. It is said, Whitefield was describing the perils of a poor blind beggar, groping his way on the edge of a precipice. Chesterfield had followed the preacher till he had brought the man out upon the giddy edge, and there his little dog abandoned him and his cane slips from his weak grip and disappears over the darkness of the cliff, and as the blind beggar totters there back and forth, Lord Chesterfield could see the man toppling over and rising from his chair in excitement he exclaimed: 'Good God, he's gone!'"[11]

On another occasion Whitefield while was using an illustration he cupped his hand to his mouth and looking upward he called out,

---

[11] E. A. Johnston, "George Whitefield A Definitive Biography In Two Volumes in One," Paperback, (Gainesville: The Old Paths Publications, 2023), p 1119.

"Gabriel, Gabriel! Have you any Methodists up there?" "No, Methodists up here", the angelic replied. "Gabriel, Gabriel! Have you any Presbyterians up there?" "No Presbyterians up here." "Gabriel, Gabriel! Have you any Baptists up there?" "No, no Baptists up here. All we have here are Christians washed in the Blood of the Lamb!"

When one examines the sermons of D. L. Moody you will find that over fifty percent of Moody's sermons were illustrations. One of the reasons Moody could hold the attention of 10,000 at a time for a month at a time in great cities such as London, Edinburgh, and Glasgow, was the interest produced by the illustrations in his sermons.

As a preacher, it is vastly important to include illustrations throughout one's sermon to hold interest and stir emotion. A good example of this is a sermon by Sam Jones preached in the city of Nashville, TN in 1885; it was his first sermon of his campaign and he preached it to 8,000 people in a tent in downtown Nashville. Take special note how Sam Jones builds emotion in his sermon with this Civil War illustration and how his audience could relate to it personally! Here now, is that striking sermon:

"Now this incident, and I am through. We all love bravery. Ah, there is not a man living who does not admire a brave man, though he is his enemy.

"I want to refer to an incident of this last war. I am sorry about that war—sorry we ever fired on the old Union flag. I was too young, but if I had been old enough, I would have gone with my father and brother and my six uncles and fought with all my might. But I will tell you this much—there is not a man who walks the American soil today that would fight for the old Stars and Stripes any quicker than I would this minute (Applause). God knows my heart. I am loyal to the flag that floats over America, as I loyal to the banner of Jesus Christ. (Applause). But during this last war, you know when Sherman pushed his forces through Georgia, and when Johnston surrendered his forces in Atlanta into the hands of General

Hood, that brave Southern general, who died since the war—a braver man never drew sword in battle—General Hood brought Johnston's army, you recollect back through North Georgia and into Tennessee, after Sherman drove Johnston to Atlanta. There Hood took charge of the Southern forces and came back into Tennessee. You recollect that memorable battle of Franklin, Tennessee. This instance, not historical, but in many respects true, illustrates just what I want to say to you.

"At the battle of Franklin, General Hood had his tent pitched upon a prominence, and he could overlook the whole battle to his right. As you remember, he had already lost one of his legs. While the battle was waging hot and thick, General Hood was limping up and down in front of the tent, and whenever he would turn and face the battle, he saw that there was a fort in a locust grove the Union forces held, and that fort was sending forth shot and shell and death into his own ranks. As he walked up and down in front of his tent, and every time he turned around, would see this volley of shell and death as it hewed down his ranks, and he watched the volley from that fort, and directly he called his adjutant-general.

"Adjutant-general, come here. The adjutant-general loped up on his horse, and General Hood said, 'Adjutant-general, go and present my compliments to General Cleburne, and tell him, I ask at his hands the fort in the locust grove.' The adjutant-general loped off down to where General Cleburne's division of corps was, and asked for General Cleburne. They said, 'He is missing; he has not been seen in two hours. We think he is killed.' The adjutant-general loped back to General Hood and said: 'General Cleburne is missing. They think he is killed. They don't know where he is.'

"General Hood dropped his head and walked up and down in front of his tent, and every time he would turn, he would see the volley of shell and death play into his ranks. Again, calling his adjutant-general to him, he said, Adjutant-general, go and present my compliments to General Cheatham, and tell him, I ask at his hands the fort in the locust grove.' The adjutant-general loped off down to General Cheatham's quarters, and they said, 'General Cheatham is not here; he is missing. He many have been killed.' The adjutant-general hurried back and said, 'they think General Cheatham is killed also.'

"General Hood commenced marching up and down, and every time he turned, he saw that fort as it threw out its shell and death. He stopped again, and said, 'Adjutant-general.'

"His adjutant-general came up to him, then he said, 'Adjutant-general, go and present my love (no compliments about this—go and present my love) to General Cockrell, and tell him I ask at his hands that fort in the locust grove.' The adjutant-general went down to General Cockrell's division and said, 'General Cockrell, General Hood presents his love, and asks at your hands that fort in the locust grove.'

"General Cockrell straightened himself on the saddle, cast his bright eye down the line, and said, 'First Missouri Brigade, Attention!' and dropped his finger on the fort. And they charged with a fearful loss on that fort, and captured it! And silenced the guns. And Cockrell called his adjutant-general and said, 'Adjutant-general, go and present my love to General Hood, and tell him I also present him the fort in the locust grove. '

"Brethren, of Nashville, at this hour, as adjutant-general of the Lord Jesus Christ, I point my finger at the citadel of sin in Nashville, and tell you that my Lord and Saviour presents you all His love, and He asks at your hands this fort that is desolating so many hearts. And I hope that in less than one month from today I can say, 'Blessed Christ, Nashville presents her love to you, and also presents you the whole city saved by the precious blood.' (Cries of 'Amen') O Lord, grant it. And I want every man and woman here today that wants to join in the warfare against sin, whether you are in the church or not, if you would be on the right side and try to win the city to Christ. I want every one that would see the city presented to God stand up. Let everyone stand up that says, 'I am in for bringing the whole city to Christ.' (Nearly the whole congregation arose). Well, thank God, we have thousands. Very few sitting, and thousands standing up and saying, 'We will take the fort for Christ.'"[12]

---

[12] E. A. Johnston, "Sam Jones A New Biography", (Gainesville: The Old Paths Publications, 2023). pp 90-94.

The right use of illustrations can make any sermon memorable. It is beneficial to preaching to use proper illustrations to bring out the text and drive the central truth of the Scripture home. Remember, sermons and illustrations go hand in hand like biscuits and gravy!

CHAPTER SIXTEEN
SAMPLE SERMONS

"Churches like Samson, have gone to sleep in the lap of Delilah, and though they go forth Sunday after Sunday to shake themselves, the Spirit of the Lord has departed. Samson may have looked better after he had his hair cut, but he lost his power."

Vance Havner

It is important to study sermons. Particularly "revival sermons". I have spent hours reading the sermons of men like Soloman Stoddard, Thomas Brooks, Jonathan Edwards. I highly recommend the reading of the sermons of the Puritans—they still have lightning and thunder!

The following sermons are from my book, *"Sermons For Revival"*, and as you study them notice how they are structured, what the centralizing theme is, and how the Scripture passages chosen are nails which fasten the hearer to the message. Each of these sermons can be listened to on my SermonAudio website: Evangelism Awakening, E. A. Johnston.

SERMON NUMBER ONE
"AMERICA: REVIVAL OR RUIN"

Bible Text: Amos Chapter Four.

Downloads: 20,930.

Preached on: Wednesday, July 25, 2012.

When I was a little boy in the 1950's, things were different in America back then. I remember this country when Hollywood had censors, politicians had a conscience, and America had a moral compass. Hemlines were lower and morals were higher and sin was called sin and not social disorders. Of course, we didn't' have the technology that we have today. Back then if you said Microsoft they thought you were referring to your mattress. And we didn't have Wi-Fi. We had hi-fi. It was a time when only women wore earrings and only sailors had tattoos. I remember America when it still had a strong work ethic and business abounded in honesty and integrity and a man's word and handshake was as good as gold. And I remember in America when a parent did not have to worry about what their children saw on TV and marriage was between a man and a woman. There was such a thing as shame in society back then.

I remember America when the church still had authority and there was still a fear of God in the land. I remember a nation that stood on biblical principles and looked to God for guidance and to the church for direction. It was okay to pray in public school back then and the Ten Commandments were publicly displayed. And if any atheist cried out against it, there were more than enough Christians to shout that person down because God had the majority in the nation back then. And I remember an America that was looked up to by other nations and we were a country that held on to the principles of our founding fathers and Old Glory was never stomped on and set on fire because we respected too much what it stood for. Back then there was such a thing as a weekly prayer meeting in the church and people actually came to pray. And they weren't embarrassed to cry when they prayed and they prayed loud and long and did so until they grabbed hold of God and the fire fell and consumed the sacrifice. The church back then didn't operate on money and manpower, but by God and Holy Ghost power. Back then the church influenced society instead of society influencing the church. And I remember preachers who preached about the blood and the cross and they warned that hell was hot and a future judgment awaited all mankind. Those kind of preachers weren't afraid of men, but they sure feared the Almighty.

I keep using the word remember because all I have is my memory of these former things. Today America is facing ruin and only a heaven-sent revival will save this nation from complete destruction.

You see, Christianity was always meant to be counter-cultural. In the New Testament, when the church met the world, there was a clash because the church went in one direction and pagan society went in the other. Now they travel side by side and there is just a rub between them.

We wanted to reach the world so we brought the world into the church. Where has that gotten us? It has only corrupted the house of God. When the people of God begin to drift away from the heart of God, then God will send remedial judgments to call His people back to Him.

My message today is entitled, "America: Revival or Ruin." It is about the remedial judgments of God and we want to begin in the book of Amos, chapters 3 and 4.

Amos was a fiery prophet of God whose main message was judgment. God's timetable was up and the people of God would not return to Him, so He sent a series of judgments upon them; remedial judgments, each one being stronger and harsher than the previous one. God was seeking to get their attention, but they refused to listen. Is God seeking to get our attention today? Is America under the chastisement of the Almighty? Have we not turned our backs on God in this country today?

You know, 9/11 was a wake up call, but almost everyone went back to sleep. God is still in His mercy, seeking to get our attention. But the timetable is quickly running out. This is the most critical time in the history of this nation, because if things don't drastically change and there is a turning of this nation back to God, then there will be no nation to turn. It will be gone.

Look at ancient Rome and their military might that ruled the world with an iron fist. Can you fear an Italian army today? No. it is laughable. America is now laughable in the eyes of the world.

Well, look in your Bibles at Amos chapter 3, verse 3. What does it say? "Can two walk together, except they be agreed?" Can you walk with God and still hang on to your wretched sins? Can you name the name of Christ and live like the devil? If you want to walk with God you must turn from your sins and pursue a life of holiness. God is holy. God's Word declares, "Follow…holiness without which no man shall see the Lord" (Hebrews 12:14).

The problem with Israel here in Amos was that they had quit walking with God. They preferred their sins over God. They turned their back side to God. And yet they still believed they were alright in God's eyes; that God had somehow adjusted Himself to their wicked ways; that He tolerated their sins because of His great love for them. God was angry with the Jews and God is angry with the church member who claims to be a Christian yet who still hangs on to his sins.

"Can two walk together, except they be agreed?" Can they?

Picture in your mind the story of Elijah and his contest with the prophets of Baal on Mount Carmel. He was up against 450 prophets of Baal; remember that? Elijah built an altar and challenged the prophets of Baal to call on their gods to consume the sacrifice and their gods didn't show up. Finally, Elijah began to mock them and said that perhaps their god was on vacation. But listen to what Elijah said to the assembled crowd that day. "And Elijah came unto all the people, and said, *How long halt ye between two opinions? If the LORD be God, follow him, but if Baal, then follow him. And the people answered him not a word*" (1 Kings 18:21).

In other words, if you want to walk with God, you can't have one foot with God and with the other play footsie with the world. Notice he said, *"if the LORD be God."* Is Jesus your Lord or is He just your insurance policy against hell?

In Amos chapter 3, verse 6 the text reads: *"shall there be evil (calamity) in a city, and the LORD hath not done it?"*

Never in my lifetime have there been so many frequent natural disasters in this country, one right after another. What do you think that is? Is it global warming or mother nature? Or is it God allowing Satan to wreak havoc on our society and on our land? In the book of Job, Satan brought a great wind to collapse the house of Job and remove his family and his wealth. God gave Satan permission to do it. Satan is not on the same level as God. There is not an equal war between good and evil. Satan is only a created being; a judged created being whose time is short and he knows it. The last days will be so terrible you will not want to be alive if God does not send revival.

Let us now look at how God sends remedial judgments to a people who have turned their backs on Him. Look at Amos chapter 4 beginning in verse 6: *"And I also have given you cleanness of teeth in all your cities, and want of bread in all your places; yet have ye not returned unto me, saith the LORD."*

Judgment number one was that God sent a famine in the land. In His mercy He sent them a famine. But how did they respond? *"Yet have ye not returned unto me, saith the LORD."*

Well, look at judgment number two in verse 7. It is more severe: *"And also I have withholden the rain from you, when there were yet three months to the harvest: and I caused it to rain upon one city, and caused it not to rain upon another city: one piece was rained upon, and the pierce whereupon it rained not withered."*

See, you can go a week without food, but man cannot live long without water. God sent a drought to His disobedient people. Now do they turn back to Him and repent and seek His face? No. *"...yet have ye not returned unto me."*

You see, back then the local Jewish weather man told them it was just mother nature acting up again. They would just have to grin and bear it. But they didn't return to God. So He brings an even more severe judgment. Look at judgment number three in verse 9: *"I have smitten you with blasting and mildew, when your gardens and your vineyards and your fig trees and your olive trees increased, the palmerworm devoured them: yet have ye not returned unto me, saith the LORD."*

God sent a financial collapse. Our economy is growing worse and worse and a global depression is on the horizon. Have we turned back to God? God is seeking to get our attention. Are we paying attention or are we asleep? The remedial judgments of God when unheeded become the increasing judgments of God.

Look at how severe judgment number four is. Look at verse 10: *"I have sent among you the pestilence after the manner of Egypt; your young men have I slain with the sword, and have taken away your hoses; and I have made the stink of your camps to come up unto your nostrils; yet have ye not returned unto me, saith the LORD."*

He has removed the young men of the city by death. You know, take the young men out of a community and the community has little future. God sent death to them through pestilence and war. What is it going to take in America? What kind of terrible national calamity will have to fall upon this nation before it turns back to God? Will it ever turn back to God? When the Christian leaders refuse to acknowledge that God is judging America and judging the churches in America, then we have the blind leading the blind.

Pastors of former generations were wiser and preached revival sermons to turn the hearts of the people back to God. Listen to a sermon preached by a leading pastor in Boston in 1755 when an earthquake shook that city. Listen to the title of his sermon:

"Earthquakes the works of God and tokens of his just displeasure being a discourse on that subject wherein a particular description of this awful event of Providence made public at this time on occasion of the late dreadful earthquake which happened on the 18th of November 1755."

The text of the sermon was Psalm 18:7, *"Then the earth shook and trembled; the foundations also of the hills moved and were shaken, because he was wroth."*

The leading pastors in New England all preached similar sermons at that time. They called the congregations to fast and pray and repent of their sins and fall on their faces before the God of terrible majesty. Even the President of the United States had a fear of God back then and called the entire nation to a time of humiliation before an offended Creator. Consider this notice in a newspaper from 1798. "A discourse delivered in the First Presbyterian Church of Philadelphia on Wednesday, May 9, 1798, recommended by the President of the United States to be observed as a day of fasting, humiliation and prayer throughout the United States of America."

How much more urgent is the great need for America today? We can't look to the White House to help us. We can't even look to the church house to help us. Who will take a stand for God in this land today? Who? It is time for the people of God to turn from their wicked ways and fast and pray and seek His holy face in repentance and humiliation or there will not be a nation left to pray in. when will the churches in the land stop playing church and get right with God and call a time of solemn assembly where the people of God cry out to God in nights of desperation and prayer? Why complain about the direction of this nation when you are not willing to do anything about it? God says, "Return unto me, and I will return unto you" (Malachi 3:7).

How bad do we want Him? Listen to this warning from the book of Romans:

> *"The night is far spent, the day is at hand: let us therefore cast off the works of darkness, and let us put on the armour of light. Let us walk honestly, as in the day: not in rioting and drunkenness, not in chambering and wantonness, not in strife and envying. But put ye on the Lord Jesus Christ, and make not provision for the flesh, to fulfil the lusts thereof"* (Romans 13:12-14).

Let me tell you what can happen to a church. Things can get between you and God. Leonard Ravenhill used to tell a story about a friend of his who was on fire for God. Every time Ravenhill got around this man he was more thirsty for Christ and things of eternal worth. Do you know people like that, people that make you thirsty for God? Well, this man was like that. Every time he got around him he wanted to talk about Jesus and winning souls. Then one day he began collecting stamps. As his collection grew, so did his enthusiasm for stamp collecting. Leonard Ravenhill said, "This man called me up one day and said, 'Come on over and I will show you my new stamp collection of British colonials that cost me $50,000." Ravenhill said that pretty soon this man no longer wanted to talk about Jesus or the things of God. He just wanted to talk about stamps. A harmless little thing like a stamp drew that man away from God.

What is it with you? What is the thing, no matter how seemingly harmless, that has stolen your affection from Jesus? Why is your Bible a closed book? Why is your prayer life so stale and so infrequent? Why is your walk so up and down?

You see, a church has influence for God in a community as long as the church members have influence with God. A church is only a reflection of its members. The members of a church will either draw people to God like a magnet or turn people away from Him by their inconsistent and worldly lives.

Let me share a story with you. A traveling preacher was passing through a certain city, and he wanted to go by and visit a historic church that had a long reputation for doing good for the Lord. But when he got into town, he stopped at a local restaurant to grab some lunch and ask directions to that famous church. The owner of the restaurant was well familiar with that church and when the traveling preacher went on and on about all the great things that church had done, the owner of the restaurant looked at him strangely and commented, "Yes, it used to be that way some time ago. If you want directions to that church go up the road a piece and turn right at the next stop sign. Then go up a hill and at the top of the hill there will be a sign telling you the way to that church." "What does the sign say?" asked the traveling preacher. The man paused and with a sad look said, "The sign says, Caution, children at play."

I am sorry to say I have known churches like that, too many, that once did great things for God, that God did great things through them, and now there are signs out front that say, "Caution, children at play."

The hour is late, friends. It is time to get serious with God. Get serious with God and

God will get serious with you. If your free time is spent on anything other than prayer and Bible study and things of eternal worth, I feel sorry for you. There is a bema seat for believers. And there we will receive gold, silver, and precious stones or wood, hay, and straw. When the works of your life pass through the fire what will remain? Will it be gold, silver, and precious stones? Will your life for Christ shine like a brilliant jewel reflecting His glory? Or will you stand there knee deep in the ashes of a wasted life and bend over and press those ashes into His nail-pierced hand? Do you want to be found playing with the marbles of the world when Jesus appears at the rapture? If we really believe we are living in the last days, our lives don't reflect it. If we really believed that Christ is returning soon, we would not be so consumed with this world. Some of you within the sound of my voice may be living your last years. How do you want to spend them? Chasing a little white ball around a golf course? I used to do that until God showed me what golf stood for—Golden Opportunities Lost Forever.

What occupies your time? Are we redeeming the time because the days are evil? You may think I am morbid, but I read the obituaries every day. I take time to read each one and contemplate on their life and how they lived it. "He was an avid golfer. He loved to ride motorcycles. He had a passion for bowling and he was a deacon at such and such Baptist church."

Seldom do I read an obituary about a man that says he had a passion for God and was consumed with thing of eternal worth. He lived to bring the lost in. he loved Jesus with his whole heart. No, it usually he loved his antique cars, or his bass boat, and so on. I read an obituary recently about a church member whose friend wrote the article and said the deceased loved martinis.

Like I said, you can learn a lot about a person by what consumes their time here on earth. My late mentor, Dr. Stephen F. Olford, used to quote, "Only one life, 'twill soon be past. Only what's done for Christ will last."

But, I repeat, only a heaven-sent revival will save America from ruin. These are, indeed, the end times. Do you believe that? And the end is drawing closer and closer every day. We are living in the day of the spirit of Antichrist right now. Our society grows darker and darker with each new day. You'd better forget about your theory of relax and be raptured. I believe in the rapture of the church, but I believe the American church is going to through fire and persecution before Christ comes again. Persecution is on the way to America and it is right around the corner. The chaff will be separated from the wheat.

But there is hope of revival for America. The Word of God gives us a pathway to revival. It is found in 2 Chronicles, chapter 7and verse 14:

> *"If my people, which are called by my name, shall humble themselves, and pray, and seek my face, and turn from their wicked ways; then will I hear from heaven, and will forgive their sin, and will heal their land."*

Let me ask you a question. Does our land need healing? Let me ask you the next question. Are you willing to pay the price for revival and really do what the verse says and get serous with God and humble yourselves before Him, pray and seek His face in these dark days? And are you willing to do the last part of this verse which God requires from us? And that is to turn from your wicked ways? Are you willing to repent of your sins and come clean with God not only for your sake and the sake of your family, but for the sake of our nation? For the nation is merely the reflection of its people. America used to be a God-fearing nation because the Christians used to fear God and live holy lives toward Him. We are to be salt, the Bible says. You see, salt is a preservative. We are to a a preservative from evil for this nation to do good for the glory of God.

Listen friends, God promises us in His Word, *"Return unto me, and I will return unto you"* (Malachi 3:7). Are we willing to do it with a sincere heart? The passage in Second Chronicles mentions duties on our part that we must do to gain the ear of the Almighty. I believe the average church member is willing to do the first two aspects of this text, humble themselves and pray. But very few are willing to comply with the most solemn aspect of this text, and that is repent and turn from their wicked ways.

Listen to me. God will not move one skinny inch until we comply with His demands of repentance on our part. If we humbly seek His face in prayer and supplication and turn from our wicked sways, He then promises to do two big things for us, hear and heal. This is an if/then proposition in Scripture. If the people of

God will do such and such, then God will do such and such. God says that if my people do these things, then I will hear their prayers and heal their land.

You see, there was revival in the days of Hezekiah because he complied with the precepts of 2 Chronicles 7:14. King Hezekiah gathered his religious leaders together and told them, *"Hear me, ye Levites, sanctify now yourselves, and sanctify the house of the LORD God of your fathers, and carry forth the filthiness out of the holy place"* (2 Chronicles 29:5).

Hezekiah was instructing them to do two things. Number one, clean the temple of its idols and, number two, clean the altar of their hearts in repentance. We see this in 2 Chronicles chapter 29 and verses 15 through 16. Listen to what the people of God did in response to the king's request of getting right with God. The text reads:

> *"And they gathered their brethren, and sanctified themselves, and came, according to the command-ment of the king, by the words of the LORD, to cleanse the house of the LORD. And the priests went into the inner part of the house of the*

LORD, to cleanse it, and brought out all the uncleanness that they found in the temple of the LORD into the court of the house of the LORD. And the Levites took it, to carry it out abroad into the brook Kidron."

This is what the people of God did. They searched the temple to find unclean idols and then brough them out, took them to the brook Kidron, and burned them there. they sanctified themselves and God brought a mighty revival under King Hezekiah because he did that which was right in the sight of the Lord.

It is up to the church in America today to so the same: to search our sanctuaries to see what idols we have set up which displease and grieve God and take those worldly idols back out of our churches and get rid of them. Then we are to search our hearts under the bright spotlight of the Holy Spirit to see if there is anything grievous to God in our lives and turn from it in repentance. Then, and only then, will our prayers have power with God to the degree that He will indeed hear and heal: hear our prayers and heal our land.

You know, we don't hear much preaching today on the cross in the life of the believer. But if we want God to hear us and to take us seriously, we must crucify anything in our lives that is displeasing to Christ Jesus. When we get serious with God, He will get serious with us and answer our prayers and bring a Holy Ghost revival to America that will shake the gates of hell from coast to coast.

This is a call to fall on our faces and seek Him in sincerity of heart. Will we do it? Will we do it? America: revival or ruin. Will we heed the warnings? God help us if we don't.[13]

---

[13] E. A. Johnston, "Sermons For Revival", (Gainesville: The Old Paths Publications, 2023), pp13-21.

SERMON NUMBER TWO
"A TOUR OF HELL"

Bible Text: Luke 16:23.

Downloads: 11,384

Preached On: Wednesday, July 25, 2012

When I was a little boy I visited a museum in Chicago and in that museum was an exhibit which fascinated me. it was called, "The Coal Mine" and it was like an amusement park ride. You got into an elevator and it gave you the sensation of going deep into the ground to a coal mine. The elevator became darker and colder and the walls of the elevator moved so you believed you were descending deep into the bowels of the earth. All your sensations told you that you were going deep into a coal mine beneath the ground.

Today I'm going to be your tour guide and escort you into the nether regions underground. For I'm going to take you on a tour of hell. We don't' hear much about hell these days and many do not believe in a literal hell. But Jesus did and that's good enough for me. Amen?

I bring this message for two reasons. Number one, to bring glory to the Father.

Number two, to warn those outside of Christ to flee from an eternal punishment called hell and to seek refuge in your only hope, Jesus Christ.

Our text today is from Luke, chapter 16 and verse 23:

> *"And in hell he lift up his eyes, being in torments."*

You see, friends, hell is a place of torments; a place of everlasting burnings where the worm dieth not. I must issue a disclaimer there before we proceed on this tour of hell. This message is not for the faint of heart but it is for the stony heart. People must be warned of hell.

What happens to persons when they die? Is it just a blank void of nothingness? Is there some kind of life after death? Some people believe in reincarnation where a person gets several chances in life to get it right. But my Bible says we only have one life to live and after that we face the Judge of all the earth.

This is what it says in Hebrews: *"And as it is appointed unto men once to die, but after this the judgment"* (9:27). When a believer dies, he or she goes to heaven to be with Jesus. My Bible tells me that to be absent from the body is to be present with the Lord. When an unbeliever dies, they awake in a terrible place called hell.

There is a book I read about hell that was written by a cardiologist at the UT School of Medicine in Tennessee. His name is Dr. Maurice Rawlings. He was an avowed atheist until he witnessed some near death experiences of his patients, patients who had been clinically dead on the operating table. They had come back to life and what these patients experienced during that time of death startled Dr. Rawlings. Some of his patients went to hell and back; hence the title of his book, "To Hell and Back".

What he witnessed in these patients disturbed him because their faces would be twisted in a grimace of terror. At times they would shriek in horror and cry out in agony and their eyes would dilate as they described horrific scenes of tortured souls and a burning hell. This so shocked Dr. Rawlings that he began to wonder if there really was a heaven and hell after all. So he began to study the Bible and what it said about hell and the afterlife. Through his study he got saved and became a Christian and he wrote several books on the topic of hell and its torments.

We don't hear much preaching today on the subject of hell. You know, old time preachers used to preach on hell often to awaken the lost to see their real condition and perilous position outside of Christ. But we preach nice little messages today that don't disturb anybody. Well, Jesus preached about hell and warns us not to go there. See, there's an invisible world all around us.

There's a story about Charles Spurgeon, the famous British preacher. Spurgeon was in a hotel room in France where he lay dying. His close friend and aide, Joseph Harrold, related the following story. He said, that as he gazed out the hotel window toward the hills beyond, under a cloudless sky, he was astonished at what he saw. To his dying day Joseph Harrold claimed he saw, out on the hillside that day, a company of angels hovering above the hills looking as though they were waiting for someone. They did not have long to wait. Spurgeon died shortly thereafter.

I believe that. I believe that when we die as believers, angels take us up to heaven. Does not Jesus Himself say so? In our passage of Scripture today from Luke's gospel, the Lord Jesus is describing the beggar, Lazarus, who dies, and Jesus said, "And it came to pass, that the beggar died, and was carried by the angels into Abraham's bosom" (16:22).

I believe that. I also believe that when an unsaved person dies, demons drag that person down to hell.

Come with me now as we descend into the nether regions and see what the Bible has to say about the existence of a literal hell. This is what the Bible says, hell is a place of punishment for sin, hell is inhabited by demons, hell is an abode for the wicked dead, and hell is a place of eternal suffering.

Let's look at the first of these: hell is a place of punishment for sin. The fact that God punishes sin is found throughout God's Word. My Bible states that God is angry with the wicked every day. Look at the biblical record. In Genesis we find the following evidence that God punishes sin:

"And GOD saw that the wickedness of man was great in the earth, and that every imagination of the thoughts of his heart was only evil continually. And it repented the

LORD that he had made man on the earth, and it grieved him at his heart. And the LORD said, I will destroy man whom I have created from the face of the earth" (Genesis 6:5-7).

In the biblical record found again in Genesis we see that God will punish sin. God told Abraham that He would destroy wicked inhabitants of Sodom and Gomorrah. The Bible record says, "Because the cry of Sodom and Gomorrah is great, and because their sin is very grievous" (18:20). And the Word of God proves that a holy God will punish sin, for the text reads, "Then the LORD rained upon Sodom and upon Gomorrah brimstone and fire, from the LORD out of heaven. And he overthrew those cities, and all the plain, and all the inhabitants of the cities and that which grew upon the ground" (19:24-25).

See, the trouble with our society today is that people sleep well at night because they don't believe God will punish sin. Even many church members today don't believe in a God that will punish sin. They do not believe in that kind of God, their God wouldn't act that way and send people to hell. But listen, friends, the God of the Bible will, because the God of the

Bible punishes sin. But some church members don't let their profession of faith interfere with their daily living because they just don't believe God will punish sin. And no one will be interested in what Christ did on the cross until they believe God will punish sin.

We have forgotten what the message of the gospel is. In your day and mine, in our generation, we are fed a diluted gospel message of the cross that speaks only about an offered Christ, but there is no use to offer a remedy to people who don't' need a remedy. There is no use to preach the second message of the cross , the forgiveness of sin through Christ's blood. Listen, friend, this generation doesn't think it needs its sins forgiven; they just don't think there is any need. But we still go on and only offer the second message of the cross; Christ and His forgiveness of sins. However, this generation of hell bound sinners needs to hear the "first" message of that bloody cross and that message is, God will punish sin. Every time they nailed those nails into the flesh of the Son of God, every stroke of the hammer said, **GOD WILL PUNISH SIN. GOD WILL PUNISH SIN. GOD WILL PUNISH SIN!**

But in our day of weak evangelism, we beg people to come to Jesus, but they don't feel like they need Him. A man won't go to the doctor unless he discovers he's deathly ill. When a man is sick to the point of death and the doctor has a remedy that will cure him, that man will give that doctor every cent he has to get well and live. But he doesn't need a cure if he doesn't think he's sick.

Listen to me, dear ones. If you do not hear anything else I say today, remember this; **God will punish sin**. That's the first message of the cross and after somebody believes that you can come in with the second message of the cross; that substitute who hangs there in my stead. Christ is God's sacrifice and my substitute.

So the first thing you need to accept on this tour of hell is the fact that hell is a place of punishment for sin. People go to hell because God sends them there to punish them for sin. People do not send themselves to hell; that's a ridiculous statement. Listen, Jesus hung on a bloody cross for sinful man. God was reconciling the world through the death of His Son. Jesus said that men are cast into hell:

"Wherefore if thy hand or thy foot offend thee, cut them off, and cast

them from thee: it is better for thee to enter into life halt or maimed, rather than having two hands or two feet to be cast into everlasting fire" (Matthew 18:8).

Hell itself exists because of sin. Hell is a place of punishment for sin. Sin is not sent to hell but sinners are sent to hell to be punished for their sins and rebellion against a holy God who hates sin so much He cannot look upon it. That's why God looked away from His precious Son on the cross and Jesus cried out, *"My God, my God, why hast thou forsaken me?"* (Matthew 27:46).

Jesus took our sins and took the wrath of God upon Himself. For those who believe in Him shall not see death but have everlasting life. Listen, *"He that believeth not the Son shall not see life; but the wrath of God abideth on him"* (John 3:36). The wrath of God. God will pour out His wrath on those Christless individuals in hell for all eternity.

Well, let's continue our tour of hell and notice this, that hell is inhabited by demons. When I was a teenager my family moved into a haunted house. There was an evil presence in that house. Right after we moved in, my parents and I were sitting in the living room and upstairs above us we heard very strong footsteps walking down th hall. We looked at each other in alarm and my father tried to laugh it off by saying, "Spooks!" But it was not laughing matter and it happened again and again. We came to accept the fact that our house was haunted.

One night we were sitting downstairs in the living room, we heard those heavy footsteps walking up and down the hall upstairs and I ran upstairs to see if there was an intruder up there. But there was no one there, at least no one I could see. It was an eerie feeling.

But even worse than that, occasionally in the house something horrible and frightening would occur, and suddenly without warning. There was a door beneath the stairwell upon which, without warning, a loud pounding would begin on that closed door so loud it would startle you and stop you in your tracks. After that loud pounding one day I slowly crept over to that door and I grabbed the crystal doorknob and yanked the door open and I felt cold air rush out on me even though it was a hot summer day and our AC was out. Demons inhabited that house. There was an unseen evil presence there. I sure was glad when we finally moved away.

Hell is inhabited by demons. In hell you will be surrounded by demon entities and you will not be able to get away from them; but they will brush up against you, tear you, and attack you, and there will be no one to help you. Not only will you not be able to move away from them, rather you will be at their mercy. That hell is inhabited by demons is seen from the words of Christ: *"Then shall he say also unto them on the left hand, Depart from me, ye cursed, into everlasting fire, prepared for the devil and his angels"* (Matthew 25:41).

Several of the patients of Dr. Rawlings, the cardiologist, spoke of seeing demons in hell in their near-death experience. They described them as dark, shrouded entities, slimy and disfigured, grotesque in appearance and smell. These demon entities were the first ones you saw in hell. In Dr. Rawling's book, *"Beyond Death's Door,"* he writes about it in a chapter called, "Descending to Hell." He writes the description of what his patients saw there. he describes the experience of a patient apparently dying with a heart attack and coming back to life. She attended church every

Sunday and considered herself an average Christian. These are her words:

> "I remember getting short of breath and then I must've blacked out. then I saw that I was getting out of my body. The next thing I remember was entering this gloomy room where I saw in one of the windows this huge giant with a grotesque face that was watching me. Running around the windowsill were little imps or elves that seemed to be with this giant. The giant beckoned me to come with him. I didn't want to go but I had to. Outside was darkness but I could hear people moaning all around me. I could feel things moving about my feet. As we moved on through this tunnel or cave things were getting worse. I remember I was crying. Then for some reason the giant turned me loose and sent me back. I felt I was being spared."

Not only is hell inhabited by demons, but as we go deeper into this tour of hell we see it is also an abode for the wicked dead. Psalm 9, verse 17 tells us, *"The wicked shall be turned into hell, and all the nations that forget God."* Hell is crowded right now with wicked individuals. Think of all of mankind that have died since the beginning of civilization. The wicked in each generation have been cast into hell—all the idolaters and adulterers, drunkards and atheists, thieves and murderers. The most vile of humankind are in hell right now. Hitler is there, serial killers are there, rapists are there, perverts are there. All of the wicked who were on earth in the days of Noah are there. The inhabitants of Sodom and Gomorrah are there. The evil Roman emperors are there. Hell is crawling with the refuse of mankind. God-haters and every sociopath from every generation of man are there. People that you would be afraid to be left in a room with will rub up against you in hell. Their sweat will get on you and there won't be a thing you can do about it. Hell is a very crowded place.

It's been estimated that eighty-three people a minute die apart from Christ. Do the math and that comes to almost 5,000 an hour. Every day 120,000 people fall into hell. That's over 800,000 a week. Every month that adds up to three million people falling into the regions of hell. Throughout the course of a year that's 40,000,000 new arrivals in hell! Let ten years go by and that comes to 400 million souls shut up in that bottomless pit to scream in agony! Now, think back in your mind of all the generations since the time of Adam and add up all the hordes of people who died apart from Christ and occupy hell right this moment. I repeat, hell is a very crowded place!

Jesus spoke of the narrow way and the broad way. Jesus said, *"Enter ye in at the strait gate: for wide is the gate, and broad is the way, that leadeth to destruction, and many there be which go in thereat. Because strait is the gate, and narrow is the way, which leadeth unto life, and few there be that find it"* (Matthew 7:13-14). Jesus calls it a strait gate because of the difficulty of the passage. If you are truly regenerate you will make the attempt to go through the strait passage, others attempt but they are quickly discouraged and get off on the easier broader road which leads to hell.

That's where the world is. There's a vast crowd on that road today. This is the road of sin, unrighteousness and disobedience. The majority travel this less demanding, wider road and they have in every generation. Few are they who travel along the narrow way of true salvation which is self-denial, mortification, and gospel obedience. Few travelers take this course; they love their sin and stay on the broad way and are led like animals into a snare and a net. Sudden death takes people away in America today through tragedy, through sudden accidents.

Listen to what the Bible says in Ecclesiastes, chapter 9 verse 12:

"For man also knoweth not his time: as the fishes that are taken in an evil net, and as the birds that are caught in the snare; so are the sons of men snared in an evil time, when it falleth suddenly upon them."

You have no guarantee of tomorrow. Our plans for the future may not be realized. You may be like the rich man of whom Jesus spoke,

"The ground of a certain rich man brought forth plentifully. And he thought within himself, saying, What shall I do, because I have no room where to bestow my fruits? And he said, This will I do: I will pull down my barns, and build greater; and there will I bestow all my fruits and my goods. And I will say to my soul, Soul, thou hast much goods

laid up for many years; take thine ease, eat, drink, and be merry. But God said unto him, Thou fool, this night thy soul shall be required of thee" (Luke 12:16-20).

Sudden death happens every day in this country—a car crash, a murder, an accident, a heart attack. Listen, God can remove you in an instant without notice and you can suddenly enter eternity. If you are truly born again, if you die you will be carried by angels into His presence, but if you are unsaved you will die in your sins and be thrown into hell. You have no guarantee of tomorrow. You are in grave danger if you have been living in known sin and living in rebellion to the God who made you. You are like the person spoken of in Ecclesiastes,

"He that diggeth a pit shall fall into it; and whoso breaketh an hedge, a serpent shall bite him" (10:8).

The Bible declares that God is a righteous judge who acts justly and by no means clears the guilty. The great danger of suddenly dying and dropping into hell should awaken everybody out of their spiritual slumber, for it is far better to repent immediately and beg for God's mercy now then to die apart from Christ and awaken to torments of the prison of hell.

Our next stop on this tour of hell is that hell is a place of eternal suffering. Physical suffering in this world eventually ends if are Christians and we are suffering a terrible slow death. When we die there's an end to that suffering. Often, we hear of a loved one who has passed away and we hear, "Well, at least they're no longer suffering. There are now with the Lord." But for the unsaved this is not so. Their suffering continues into the next world; a world of eternal misery and physical torments to which there is no relief and no end.

The following images may give you a glimpse into hell. Think of your worst fear. Think of your absolute worst fear. Some people are afraid of the dark. Well, hell is called outer darkness; there's no light there, only deep darkness. You will not be able to see your hand in front of your face, but you will be able to hear the cries of the damned all around you, you will be able to smell their putrefying burning flesh, you will be able to feel pain, and you will experience a thirst that is never quenched.

Listen, hell is lonely place. You will have no friend there to talk to; you'll not be able to get out your cell phone and send texts to one another. They are no cell phone signals in hell. You are cut off from your companions. You will long for someone to be kind to you, someone to talk to you. There'll be loneliness all around you. Hell is a lonely place of immense agony and separation.

Jesus describes hell as a place of weeping and gnashing of teeth. Weeping speaks of great loss and grief, and gnashing of teeth signifies great anger and regret. In hell you will regret the day you spurned the love of Christ; that you turned away from the invitations of the gospel, and that you did not lay hold of Christ savingly when you had a chance. You will hate the evangelist or the preacher who fed you a false gospel and told you that you were saved when you were still unconverted. His name will be a curse word to you for all eternity! You will hate yourself for not seeking Christ while He was to be found. You will hate your sins because while on earth you took pleasure in them, but in hell there is no pleasure in sin, only torment.

Listen, friends, if you die in your sins you will wake up in hell. Imagine your shock, your confusion, your tongue so dry it feels like it will fall right out of your mouth, your heart is breaking because of your foolishness and sin. But you were overtaken in hell by demons that tear at your and rend you and come again upon you and they do not stop. Your cries are drowned out by the awful shrieks around you. Look, if you went to every hospital in your city tonight and took every patient off their pain medication, and did not give them anything for pain, not even an aspirin, their cries of agony and wailing would keep your town awake tonight.

Another terrible thing about hell is the physical pain. To be burned to death is the worst way to die. It is said to be the most painful. That is why when you see a building on fire people often leap to their deaths rather than stay inside and be burned in the flames. During the tragedy of 9/11 when the Twin Towers were on fire, many leaped to their death from a hundred stories high, rather than be burned up in the flames.

But hell is everlasting burnings. The Bible declares from the book of Isaiah, *"Who among us shall dwell with the devouring fire? who among us shall dwell with everlasting burnings?"* (33:14). Hell is said to be a lake of fire. Revelation speaks to this, *"And whosoever was not found written in the book of life was cast into the lake of fire"* (Revelation 4:11). Listen, friends, hell is continual; it is an unquenchable fire. Matthew tells us, *" He will burn up the chaff with unquenchable fire"* (3:12). Jesus tells us hell is a place *"where the worm dieth not, and the fire is not quenched"* (Mark 9:44).

Once you are in hell there is no appeasing God's wrath upon you and that terrible furnace of fire which our Lord spoke of in Matthew, *"And shall cast them into the furnace of fire; there shall be weeping and gnashing of teeth"* (13:50). Listen, that furnace is terrible.

I used to work in a grocery store when I was a teenager. One of my jobs was to take the boxes that the produce came in and bring them to the back of the store and throw them into a cast iron furnace. When I would open the door to that furnace, the flame in there so hot it was a white flame. And the heat was so intense it would singe my face just to be near it!

Malachi tells us that God's anger *"shall burn as an oven; and all the proud, yea, and all that do wickedly, shall be stubble and the day that cometh shall burn them up, saith the LORD of hosts"* (4:1).

Listen, friends, in the state of Florida there is a phenomenon called sinkholes. The ground is sand and it gives way and it caves in. Entire houses have been swallowed up without warning into these deep sinkholes. If you are outside of Christ, you are sitting on a sinkhole, for beneath you is hell and its torments and only the grace of God can keep you out of hell at this moment. God could end your life this minute if He chose to, and open the ground beneath you and drag you down to hell.

We are warned by God of the danger that lies in our not surrendering to the claims of Christ and to the gospel, *"He that being often reproved hardeneth his neck, shall suddenly be destroyed, and that without remedy"* (Proverbs 29:1). If you have ignored the invitations of the gospel, you are on slippery ground.

Listen to what God says,

"To me belongeth vengeance, and recompense, their foot shall slide in due time: for the day of their calamity is at hand and the things that shall come upon them make hast" (Deuteronomy 32:35).

Listen again to what God says in His Word:

"Surely thou didst set them in slippery places: thou castedst them down into destruction. How are they brought into desolation as in a moment! they are utterly consumed with terrors" (Psalm 73:18-19).

Listen, friends, to die suddenly and wake up in hell is to be utterly consumed with terrors. Death is even called the King of Terror. I beg you, examine yourself right now. The apostle Paul warns us in 2 Corinthians, chapter 13 and verse 5. He says,

"Examine yourselves, whether ye be in the faith; prove your own selves. Know ye not your own selves, how that Jesus Christ is in you, except ye be reprobates."

I ask you now if Jesus Christ is in you. Are you truly born again? Are you washed in the blood and born of the Sprit? Do you know that your sins are forgiven? Have you been under conviction of sin? Have you ever experienced contrition with sound humiliation? Are you seeking Christ and His righteousness? Is your heart prepared to seek Him? Can you renounce your own righteousness and cast yourself upon Christ alone for salvation.

Listen, friends, I speak to you seriously today because of the words of God in Ezekiel, chapter 3, verses 18 &19. Listen to these solemn words:

"When I say unto the wicked, Thou shalt surely die; and thou givest him not warning, nor speakest to warn the wicked from his wicked ways, to save his life; the same wicked man shall die in his iniquity; but his blood will I require at thine hand. Yet if thou warn the wicked, and he turn not from his wickedness, nor from his wicked way, he shall die in his iniquity; but thou hast delivered thy soul."

Listen, I do not want your blood on my hands. I have faithfully declared to you the full counsel of God today. Repent from your sins, turn to Christ, ask Him for saving faith and believe on Him. I have given you this tour of hell today through the Scriptures with the express hope and prayer that you do not tour it in person yourself. Hell is a one stop prison with no exit doors. Once you're shut up in there you can never get out. Don't go to hell friend! Seek Christ and seek Him now!

Listen to these gospel pleas:

"Seek ye the LORD while he may be found, call ye upon him while he is near: Let the wicked forsake his way, and the unrighteous man his thoughts; and let him return unto the LORD, and he will have mercy upon him, and to our God, for he will abundantly pardon" (Isaiah 55:6-7).

"If any man thirst, let him come unto me, and drink. He that believeth on me, as the scripture hath said, out of his belly shall flow rivers of living water" (John 7:37-38).

"And the Spirit and the bride say, Come. And let him that heareth say, Come. And let him that is athirst come. And whosoever will, let him take the water of life freely" (Revelation 22:17).

My friends, listen, the gospel is for the hungry, the weary, and the thirsty. Are you hungry for Go? Are you sick and tired of your sins? Are you thirsty for Christ? Then come. There is a promise to all those who come in sincerity of heart, "All that the Father giveth me shall come to me; and him that cometh to me I will in no wise cast out" (John 6:37).

This tour of hell is over now. I pray that you will never take a tour there in person. Repent and seek Christ now. Jesus is your only hope![14]

---

[14] Ibid, pp 23-33.

SERMON NUMBER THREE
"A SILENT CHURCH IN SINFUL NATION"

Bible Text: Jeremiah 5:21-31,

Downloads: 8,468

Preached on: Tuesday, March 5, 2013.

I have a video of Martin Lloyd-Jones as he is touring England and visiting the sights where George Whitefield labored. While standing at the site of the Bell Inn where Whitefield was born, Lloyd-Jones describes the moral climate of London in the days of Whitefield and Wesley. He said that morality was at an all-time low; spirituality in the churches was almost nonexistent; and that in London every fifth house was a gin-house, and that it seemed the city itself was in a drunken debauchery and spiritual stupor. And Lloyd-Jones glares into the camera and comments, "And where was the church in all of this?"

Today in America, our situation is far more grim than in the days of Whitefield and Wesley, our national sins more multiplied. Evil increases at a rapid rate and our society slides into a sinkhole of perversion and debauchery. Our civic leaders call evil good and good evil.

God has been legislated out of our once great country. The spirit of antichrist grows in the land and I ask the same question, "Where is the church in all of this? Where is the church? She is shamefully silent amidst a sinful nation."

And that's the title of my message today, "A Silent Church Amidst a Sinful Nation." It reminds me of the days of Nazi Germany where a German pastor made the following comments about the increasing evil in his day and his failure to cry out against it. He said, "First they came for the communists and I didn't speak out because I wasn't a communist. Then they came for the socialists and I didn't speak out because I wasn't a socialist. Then they came for the trade unionists and I didn't speak out because I wasn't a trade unionist. Then they came for the Jews and I didn't speak out because I wasn't a Jew. Then they came for the Catholics and I didn't speak out because I wasn't a Catholic. Then they came for me and there was no one left to speak for me."

Dear friends, this a graphic picture of the church in America today. Evil abounds and the and the church is silent. God is systematically removed from society and the church is silent. Perversion permeates the fabric of our society and the church is silent. The government mocks God and His authority and the church is silent. The church sleeps a sleep of death and slumbers on corporate cushions of self-indulgence and soon they will come for her. Persecution is on the way to the church in America. We have missed our opportunity to cry out; we have remained silent for too long and the hour is now too late. We have been busy building our own islands and fortifying them by growing our church campuses and building a corporate environment where we can be entertained. The nation has passed the boundaries of decency and crossed the line of blasphemy against a holy God and an offended Creator. Yet the church is silent and her silence is deafening.

I can sum up the American church by this description of a recent visit to a Baptist church. The church service led off with a Hollywood video. The content was banal and offensive, yet the church laughed. The music minister laughed, the pastor laughed, the congregation laughed because they were embarrassed. I sat there looking down at the floor and my insides groaned within me. I wept inside at the state of the church in America today that has wedded Hollywood and the world with sacred things of

God. The pastor preached a doctrinally sound sermon but there was no power of the attending Holy Spirit because the Holy Spirit had been grieved away before the pastor entered the pulpit. What occurred in that church service was a religious ceremony without spiritual transformation; worship without the presence of God. We have become, as a people of God, impotent, apathetic, and indifferent. We'd rather be entertained than challenged spiritually. We have turned into a cappuccino church; all froth and no substance.

Listen to the wise words of Samuel Chadwick, a pastor of former days,

> "When a church is run on the same lines as a circus, there may be crowds but there is no Shekinah."

Oh, friends, where is the Shekinah glory in our churches today? How the glory has departed from among us and we have not even noticed. We are like Samson who left the tent and shook himself but knew not that the Spirit of God was no longer upon him.

Listen to the comments of another pastor, a godly man, W. Graham Scroggie, as he pleaded with pastors in his day.

"Make a show. The people love a show and you will gain the end of your ambition at once. The crowd is always ready for a sensation and alas there are always those who are disposed to stimulate religion, to fill the churches by the method of sensationalism."

Listen friends, to yet another man, another pastor, who was much wiser than us in his day. Listen to Alan Redpath, former pastor of the Moody Church in Chicago. Listen to his words:

"Today, the Christian church is helpless. Behind the scenes and away from the public arena, we are facing powers of darkness too strong for us because somewhere in our personal lives we have forfeited our right to the Spirit's anointing, His authority, and His power. In His absence, all we can do is to substitute planning and organization, schemes and techniques."

Alan Redpath's stinging observation can be modified for our day by adding to our substitution of God, forms of entertainment in the sanctuary of God.

Dear pastor brother, Hollywood has no place in the sanctuary of God. How can you introduce strange fire into your assembly and still have the fire of God? You cannot. These idols should be removed from the house of God. When I visit churches and see the deplorable spiritual condition of the church in America today, I weep and groan and beg God to forgive us for our spiritual slumber and dishonoring of Him. We have tried to shrink God down to our size and taken salvation out of the hands of God and placed it in the hands of man. Society crumbles all around us and there is little hope for the future of America, as we, as a nation, have filled up the cup of our iniquity before an offended God. It reminds me of the people of God in the days of Jeremiah, as described in Jeremiah, chapter 5, verses 21-31. Allow me to read this striking passage to us today.

Hear now this, O foolish people, and without understanding: which have eyes, and see not; which have ears, and hear not. Fear ye not me? saith the LORD: will ye not tremble at my presence, which have placed the sand for the bound of the sea by a perpetual decree, that it cannot pass it: and though the waves thereof toss themselves, yet can they not prevail; though they roar, yet can they not pass over it? But this people hath a revolting and rebellious heart; they are revolted and gone. Neither say they in their heart, Let us now fear the LORD our God, that giveth rain, both the former and the latter, in his season; he reserveth unto us the appointed weeks of the harvest. Your iniquities have turned away these things, and your sins have withholden good things from you. For among my people are found wicked men: they lay wait, as he that setteth snares; they set a trap, they catch men. As a cage is full of birds, so are their houses full of deceit: therefore, they are become great, and waxen rich. They are waxen fat, they shine: yea, they overpass the deeds of the wicked: they judge not the cause, the cause of the fatherless, yet they prosper; and the right of the needy do they not judge. Shall I not visit for these things? saith the LORD: shall not my soul be avenged on such a nation as this? A wonderful and horrible thing is committed in the land; The prophets prophesy falsely, and the priests bear rule by their mans; and my people love to have it so: and what will ye do in the end thereof?

What a sad, tragic picture that is of a people of God who have backslidden far away from the heart of God. Well, what did God do with such a strange people? This is what He did in the form of a severe judgment upon them as seen in Jeremiah 5:15-17:

Lo, I will bring a nation upon you from far, O house of Israel, saith the LORD: it is a mighty nation, it is an ancient nation, a nation whose language thou knowest not, neither understandest what they say. Their quiver is as an open sepulchre, they are all mighty men. And they shall eat up thine harvest, and thy bread, which thy sons and thy daughters should eat: they shall eat up thy flocks and thine herds; they shall eat up thy vines and thy fig trees: they shall impoverish thy fenced cities, wherein thou trustedst, with the sword.

God will bring a swift judgment upon America if the nation does not turn back to Him. It will be such a sudden and widespread calamity that it will be numbing in its intensity of destruction of human life. It will be such a national calamity that the government will be powerless to help anyone because they will be rendered powerless themselves. God's answer to a wonderful and horrible thing committed in the land is judgment upon a sinful and disobedient people. And I ask, "Where is the church in all of this?" Why is she silent while she still has the time to do something about it? Why, brother pastor, would you rather show Hollywood movies in your church and entertain your people rather than lead them in a time of brokenness before God in humility, in repentance and prayer? Why? Because the people love to have it so. So you give them what they want instead of what they need.

God says, "No." We have misused the time given to us in this nation of ours. We have misspent it on ourselves and our own selfish desires. Now it is time to pay the piper and we as a nation are unprepared for what is about to befall us from the hand of an offended God. "Then came they for the Jews and I didn't speak because I wasn't a Jew. Then they came for the Catholics and I didn't speak because I wasn't a Catholic. Then they came for me and there was no one left to speak for me."

"O Great God, forgive us for our national sins. Forgive America for grievously offending Thee. Forgive us of our multiplied sins. Forgive our blind leaders who lead falsely. Forgive us for our allowing our nation to be permeated and saturated with perversion. Forgive us, O Lord, for our adultery and fornications, for our idol worship. But forgive us most of all, O Lord, for forsaking Thee. We as a nation, a people, have forsaken Thee. Forgive us for corrupting the house of God with abominable things. Forgive us for mixing true worship with strange fire. Forgive us for our vast personal and corporate sins. We beseech Thee, O Great God, look down and hear our cry: we seek thy face and favor. Once again, visit us with a national revival rather than a national calamity that will come in judgment. In thy wrath remember mercy. In thy wrath, remember mercy. Come again, O Lord and fill our sanctuaries with your presence and preeminence. We pray these things in the strong name of Jesus. Amen.[15]

---

[15] Ibid, pp 35-39.

SERMON NUMBER FOUR
"TEN MISTAKES OF MODERN EVANGELISM"

Preached On: Tuesday, July 30, 2013.

When I was conducting my research on the First and Second Great Awakenings, I was shocked by the vast dissimilarity of the preaching in those days compared with the preaching of our day. I read the sermons of Jonathan Edwards and his contemporaries of the 18th century and then I studied the sermons of Asahel Nettleton and his contemporaries of the 19th century, and I noticed that God seemed to be pleased to bless the messages that were preached in those centuries with tremendous outpourings of His grace and revival and spiritual awakening. But, I look around today and all I see is deadness everywhere in the churches, and it's tied directly to the preaching of our day.

There's been a sad declension in the preaching of great doctrines of the Bible and evangelism in our day. We want to see God move in revival like He's done in former times, but the problem is, we aren't willing to preach the same messages that former men of revival preached. Part of this may be due to the fact that we're living in a day of great spiritual declension that knows little about vital Christianity. These are the days of the lukewarm church and, unfortunately, much of the preaching is lukewarm as well. It's neither hot nor cold, it's just room temperature because the pastor doesn't want to turn the temperature up in the room and upset any of his hearers. We invite a lot of people to walk an aisle and repeat a prayer but there is little evidence of true conversion in the churches in our day.

The problem with much of the evangelism is that we present a Jesus to people who aren't interested in Him because they feel they just don't need Him. Everyone needs Christ, but their eyes are blinded and they are dead in sin. Old time preachers knew how to use the Word of God to awaken sinners to their lost estate and ruined condition. After a sinner was awakened and convicted of sin by the Holy Spirit, then the remedy for sin was applied in the person of Jesus Christ. But today we offer the remedy to people who just don't realize they are sick and in need of it. We must realize that a sinner needs to be awakened before he can be converted.

But sadly, much of the preaching done today is shallow and shallow preaching leads to shallow conversions and shallow conversions lead to shallow congregations and shallow congregations leave the devil alone, leave the lost astray, and lead the nation into moral bankruptcy. So, the end result of shallow preaching is a long line of people going straight to hell.

I don't blame the White House for the problems of our hour. I don't blame the courthouse for the problems of our day. Rather, I place the blame on the pulpits of our land that have conformed to the pagan society that they were meant to reach; and instead of preaching to the lost a pure gospel of the Son of God, the pulpits water down the gospel so it can be more easily swallowed. We have swallowed this diluted gospel which lacks true spiritual nourishment, and we are sunk.

This message is a call for the pulpits of the land to return to the old paths of preaching the great doctrines of the Bible whereby men are awakened to their sins and alarmed about their lost and ruined condition before a just and holy God. My message today is entitled, "Ten Mistakes of Modern Evangelism." I will first list them and the elaborate upon each of them as we proceed.

1. Modern evangelism has tried to shrink God down go our size.
2. We have taken salvation out of the hands of God and placed it in the hands of men.
3. We fail to preach the gospel in its purity and proper order in preaching the doctrines of ruin, redemption, repentance, and regeneration.
4. There is a failure to show man his duty of repentance.
5. Modern evangelism has failed to preach the utter strictness and severity of the law of God.
6. We have failed to proclaim that man first has to be lost before he can be saved; a man needs to be awakened to see his need of Christ before the remedy can be applied.
7. Modern evangelism makes false converts by mistaking a physical act like walking an aisle and repeating a prayer as true conversion.
8. We have failed to warn sinners to flee from hell and to describe hell and its terrors.
9. We have failed to preach the Lordship of Jesus Christ.

10.   Modern evangelism has miserably failed in its portrayal of what the Christian life is to a new believer; we paint it all red roses and honey blossoms and neglect to inform our hearers about the demands of discipleship in following a crucified Savior.

Each of these ten mentioned items is of immense importance to the salvation of a soul. Things have gotten so bad in our country that when I visit churches, and I visit countless numbers of them all the time, I seldom hear what I consider to be a full presentation of the gospel message. In fact, I hear very little preaching. It's mainly teaching being done in our pulpits today. Teaching informs, preaching transforms. It is little wonder that so few are being saved today in our land because of our meager attempts to preach the true gospel message to a generation of hell-bound sinners.

MISTAKE # 1

Mistake #1: Modern evangelism has tried to shrink God down to our size. I was sitting in a large Baptist church and the minister in the pulpit made the following remark. He said, "Friends, I can't wait to get to heaven because when I die and go to heaven I'm gonna walk up to Jesus and grab his hand and shake his hand for all he has done for me." Well, I guess that seminary trained pastor was not familiar with the passage from the book of Revelation where the Apostle John encounters a risen Christ and he falls down as dead. No, this foolish minister thinks Jesus is just his pal; he can just casually walk up to the Lord of glory, grab his hand like the hand of a deacon in the hallway at church and glad hand him like he's just his buddy.

I'm afraid that this is the mentality of a majority in our pulpits today. Many have taken out their pocketknives and whittled out a god that suits them, a god they feel comfortable with, one they can worship according to their idea of him. They've tried to shrink God down to their level of reason to where He's on their level; He thinks like they do, He acts like they do. Why, He wouldn't send anybody to Hell because He just isn't like that anymore.

Our evangelism today presents a god who is our size or smaller, a far cry from the reality of the living God of the Bible, the Ancient of Days, of whom the prophet Isaiah when he caught a glimpse of Him fell down as dead and cried out, *"Woe is me!"* (Isaiah 6:5). But the god of modern-day evangelism doesn't make anybody cry out, *"Woe is me!"* because we have shrunken God down to our size so He won't intimidate anybody. But look in your Bibles and see the Jews before Mount Sinai with God's presence upon it as the mountain quaked and trembled with all smoke and fire like a great furnace, a sight so terrible that even Moses could not endure it. There are very few pulpits on a smoke today.

So, the first point is: We have shrunken God down to our size. Preachers of wiser days refer to God as the Almighty, or the Great God. Now we refer to Him on our terms and our level. This is a great mistake of modern evangelism. We must preach an exalted view of the Almighty. Isaiah 57:15 declares:

"For thus saith the high and lofty One that inhabiteth eternity, whose name is Holy: I dwell in the high and holy place, with him also that is of a contrite and humble spirit, to revive the spirit of the humble, and to revive the heart of the contrite ones."

MISTAKE #2

Mistake #2: We have taken salvation out of the hands of God and placed it in the hands of men. A favorite Bible verse of modern day evangelism is Revelation 3:20,

"Behold, I stand at the door, and knock: if any man hear my voice, and open the door, I will come in to him, and will sup with him."

This speaks of Jesus locked out of His church in the End Times through the withdrawn presence of God. He would like to come back in but the church is ignoring Him. But modern evangelists have made that verse a part of the gospel presentation and they paint an impotent Jesus standing at the door of a man's heart unable to even turn the doorknob. He is waiting helplessly like an insurance salesman with his hat in his hand, Won't you pity him and let him in? But in reality when the Christ of the Bible saves a man, He enters with authority and majesty. Man cannot save himself. Salvation is of the Lord. It is He who regenerates the heart through saving faith. And if you're saved friend, its because God gave you saving faith.

"No man can come to me, except the Father which hath sent me draw him" (John 6:44).

The orthodox revival men of the 18th and 19th centuries knew that salvation was of God, that man did not regenerate himself. Only God could transform the heart and He could give saving faith or withhold it and still be God. But, today's evangelist has taken salvation out of the hands of God and made it something you can do and it is something you can have any time you want it. I've heard preachers say, "Just open your heart and receive Jesus and He will come in."

Listen friends, a dead man cannot open his heart. Only God can open the heart of man through regeneration by His Spirit. In Acts, we read of Lydia whose heart the Lord opened (Acts 16:14). God is sovereign in salvation, yet we must not fail to call lost sinners to come to Christ. George Whitefield, with tears in his eyes, used to beg lost sinners to fly to Christ.

MISTAKE #3

Mistake #3: We fail to preach the gospel in its purity and proper order. Men like Jonathan Edwards and Asahel Nettleton knew better than most of us today. They knew that the gospel must be proclaimed in its purity and proper order. God must first be magnified and exalted. The law must be preached to show man that he's a ruined sinner under a curse and unable to help himself or alleviate his misery. That a man must be awakened to his lost condition and perilous position outside of Christ. The only way to be reconciled back to an offended God is through the blood of Christ resulting in a repentant and humble heart.

We fail today to preach up the great doctrines of ruin, redemption, repentance, and regeneration. Our Puritan fathers knew better than we today; they knew that there was a preparatory work in the sinner's heart by the Holy Spirit who acted like surgeon, bringing conviction and compunction upon the sinner's heart: conviction of sin and an awareness of it; compunction, bring a sinner to a place of humility over his sins and offending a holy Creator. Study the works of Thomas Hooker, John Shepherd, and Solomon Stoddard, to learn more about the preparatory work in the process of salvation. We, today, have made numerous false converts because of our great ignorance of how the Spirit of God works upon the sinner's heart in the act of salvation.

MISTAKE #4

Mistake #4: Failure to show man his duty of repentance. One of the greatest heresies to plague the church in the last sixty years has been the "Only Believe Gospel" invitation which omits the necessity of repentance to come savingly to Christ. Jesus declared,

"Except ye repent, ye shall all likewise perish" (Luke 13: 3,5). And thousands have entered hell from the neglect of this command.

The failure of modern day evangelism has been the neglect of the need of repentance in coming to Christ. How can one ignore God's Word which clearly states that God now commands all men, everywhere to repent. If a man does not preach faith and repentance, he's just not preaching the gospel.

We have failed as preachers to show man his duty of repentance and in the process we have cheapened the gospel and diluted it to be more palatable to sinful man. And, in the process, we have offended God. Sin is rebellion against God's authority and God will allow no rebels in His holy heaven. He will not accept you while you still have your shotgun pointed at Him! You must repent or you will surely go to hell, even if you are the chairman of the deacons!

I was at a preacher's institute in Memphis, Tennessee listening to the evangelist, Jim Wilson speak. Jim Wilson was Billy Graham's nephew. And he shared a story with us that surprised us. He said, he was up in North Carolina at the home of Billy Graham, and they were sitting on the back porch enjoying the view. This was about a year before Billy Graham went home to heaven. And Jim Wilson asked Billy Graham a searching question. He asked, "Uncle Billy. If you had to do it all over again what would you change?" and he said that Billy Graham gazed out over the distant mountain as he thought about that question. Finally, after a long pause, he answered: "I would preach repentance more." That's what the great evangelist said.

Brother preacher, we must open up the great gospel duty of repentance and show man his duty to repent toward God and be like the Apostle Paul who declared that a Christian is one who comes to God "exercising repentance toward God and faith in Jesus Christ." I fear that the "Only Believe Gospel" has filled our churches with unconverted sinners who are on the church roll but not on the Lamb's roll, the Book of Life. We must tell lost sinners it is their duty to repent now, right now, for you must repent in this world while the Spirit is striving with you for in Hell there is no repentance.

Listen, man is an enemy of God because of his sin nature and he lives in rebellion to all God stands for, and a lost sinner must throw down his shotgun of rebellion and surrender to the King of Kings and repent. Jesus said, *"For*

I am come not to call the righteous, but sinners to repentance" (Matthew 9:13). True gospel repentance involves a turning and forsaking of sin and turning to God. Jesus never preached a sinning religion but a self-crucifying one. Our churches are overrun with antinomianism because of our failure to preach man's duty of repentance.

MISTAKE #5

Mistake #5: Modern evangelism has failed to proclaim the utter strictness and severity of the law of God. Every man will be held up to God's unbending law and all will fail that test: *"For all have sinned, and come short of the glory of God"* (Romans 3:23). Men must realize their need of a Savior as a substitute for sin. At the Last Judgment, if you stand there in your own merits and God drops His plumb line of the strictness and severity of His holy law upon you the verdict will be "guilty". You must stand there in the merits of another—The Lord Jesus Christ! The law of God brings a true knowledge and conviction of sin as every mouth is stopped for there will be no excuses on That Day!

We preachers must preach the full counsel of God and to do that includes preaching up the law of God in all its strictness and severity, and we must warn men that the sentencing of the law will be carried out upon all guilty lawbreakers! When the thundering of the law is faithfully preached then men will see they are dead in trespasses and sin. Old Time preachers knew how to preach the law before grace. Both John Wesley and George Whitefield preached the law before grace. In fact, Whitefield remarked:

> "A sinner must first be brought to Mt. Sinai before he can be brought to Mt. Zion."

The preaching of the law is used by the Holy Spirit to bring conviction of sin by arousing him from his sleepy security by applying the unbending Divine Law to his conscience. When God descended atop Mount Sinai it was *"altogether on a smoke"* (Exodus 19:18). The threatening sounds of the law bring alarm to the unconverted, as he sees his proper standing as a law-breaker and guilty criminal before a holy and Just Sovereign God. The law of God is a slayer of the flesh, for all mankind has broken it through sin and all will be held accountable to its strictness and severity when God judges the works of man at His Great White Throne Judgment (Revelation 20:11-15).

We modern preachers have laid aside all the effective tools of the gospel that strip a sinner down and reveal to him his perilous condition outside of Christ's Blood! Since all have broken that law all deserve condemnation. The first message of the cross is that God is a God who must punish sin. The second message of the cross is that substitute for sin, in the Person of Christ Jesus. I know I am a sinner and I need a substitute for sin—and so do you friend, so do you!

MISTAKE #6

Mistake #6: Man must become lost before he can be saved. This is the biggest fault of modern-day evangelism—we just don't get men lost. Man must be awakened to the fact that he's lost before he can be converted. We foolishly tell people to just believe John 3:16 and they will be saved, and the believe a verse and go to hell. We get people to believe the fact of Christ's dying on a cross for us, but I fear many today just believe in the death of Christ rather than believing in the Christ who died.

Our evangelism is deficient and our watered-down presentation of the gospel is insufficient when it comes to saving men from sin and its penalty. God must get a man lost before He can save him. Men must be brought to the place where they see their ruined and hopeless condition apart from God. A sinner has to be brought face to face with the reality that he is on the wrong side of God and under the condemnation of God. He is standing in a perilous position outside of Christ, that without saving faith, he is doomed to an eternal hell. Men must be awakened to their lost condition before they can feel their need of a remedy for sin.

People just don't realize they are lost today, and when you offer them Jesus or ask them to believe John 3:16, they just don't feel there's any need for Him. They may accept your Jesus for an insurance ticket to heaven but not because they are under conviction of sin. But men must be awakened to their danger that they are ruined and lost in the world without God. God is against him because he is a sinner and rebel and an enemy of God. God can cut him down any time and send him to hell because He will have no rebels in His kingdom.

You see, friends, once a man gets lost, then he has hope. Then he can become a seeker of the Lord. Once a man gets desperate for God and realizes his great need of a Savior for sin he will seek God for salvation because he is hungry, weary, and thirsty.

MISTAKE #7

Mistake #7: We tell people they are saved because they have walked an aisle or repeated a prayer. Conversion is not a physical act we perform but a supernatural act God performs. God changes the heart of stone into a heart of flesh. Conversion is when a lost sinner experiences change. He is a new creation. God has given him a new disposition of holiness through the Holy Spirit. We are not converted by walking an aisle or repeating the Sinner's Prayer. I can't even find that in my Bible! And our great mistake of modern evangelism is when we get someone to respond to our emotional appeal and the walk an aisle to accept Jesus by performing a physical act, we then walk up to them, slap them on the back and shake their hand and tell them they are now saved and a Christian. But D. L. Moody was much wiser than us today, in his evangelistic meetings he always would counsel his volunteer workers never to tell someone they were now saved. Moody said, "Only the Holy Spirit can do that."

In Titus 3:5 we read:

"Not by works of righteousness which we have done, but according to his mercy he saved us, by the washing of regeneration, and renewing of the Holy Ghost."

True conversion occurs when a person has a principle of spiritual life implanted within by the Holy Ghost. This implantation of this divine principle is called regeneration. It is a supernatural act of God whereby God affects a work of grace upon the heart.

True conversion means a very great change has happened in a man. The whole temper of the heart is quite altered and when the saving change takes place, a man has a new appetite. New appetites for spiritual things and things of eternity, for the Spirit of God has affected a change within the person, giving him a new disposition which is described by the following verse from 2 Corinthians 5:17,

"Therefore if any man be in Christ, he is a new creature: old things are passed away; behold, all things are become new."

He is now savingly united to Christ and has entered a vital union with a living Lord. The Bible in Romans declares:

"For as many as are led by the Spirit of God, they are the sons of God. For ye have not received the spirit of bondage again to fear; but ye have received the Spirit of adoption, whereby we cry, Abba, Father. The Spirit itself beareth witness with our spirit, that we are the children of God" (8:14-16).

Our job as preachers is to preach the full counsel of God, call men and women, and boys and girls to repentance towards God and faith in Jesus Christ, and then let the Holy Spirit do His work.

MISTAKE #8

Mistake #8: We have failed miserably to warn sinners to flee from the wrath to come and preach up the terrors of hell and damnation to this lost generation. How many sermons on hell have you heard preached this year? God used men like Jonathan Edwards and Asahel Nettleton because they preached on the doctrine of hell and warned sinners not to go there. Jesus spoke of hell and its torments. He said it was a place where the worm dieth not and a place of outer darkness where there is weeping and gnashing of teeth. Weeping speaks of great loss and grief; and gnashing of teeth signifies great anger and regret

Old time preachers always preached on the agonies of hell as a means to awaken sinners to their lost condition and their danger of damnation. But today we just quote John 3:16 and think that is enough gospel to give them.

But we must warn folks about the dangers of dying in your sins. Hell is a pace of torment, of great anguish, and of unspeakable terror. Listen friend, hell is your worst nightmare come true and there is no waking up from it and no escaping of it! Once you are shut up in there you are locked up in there forever.

How foolish we modern evangelists are today to neglect the use of one of the most effective weapons in evangelism, which is preaching on the doctrine of a literal hell. Men like Edwards and Nettleton warned their hearers and God sent powerful revivals under their faithful preaching. Hell is a reality that lost sinners cannot escape and we must be faithful preachers and warn men and women and boys and girls about their need of a Savior from sin, called Jesus Christ so they won't end up in a devil's hell!

MISTAKE #9

Mistake #9: Modern evangelism has failed to preach up the Lordship of Jesus Christ. The missing doctrine in the church today is the Lordship of Jesus Christ and this is why there is so much lawlessness and insubordination among many church members today. Antinomians fill our churches and their philosophy is:

"Once saved, always saved, sin as much as I want to and still go to heaven."

The Lordship of Jesus Christ must be proclaimed because the gospel has rights and claims on all followers of Jesus. Jesus is a King, a Sovereign, and He will have none in His kingdom who are rebels against His authority. Men must throw down their shotgun of rebellion and submit to the Lordship of Christ Jesus. Self must be dethroned and another enthroned there—the Lord Jesus Christ!

Jesus sits at the right hand of the Father and He reigns in glory as Lord and He earned that right by way of a bloody cross. You must take Christ where He is right now and He's a living Lord. The biggest omission in our churches today is the missing doctrine of the Lordship of Jesus Christ. You must bow to His Lordship now or He will place His foot on your neck and make you bow to Him when His enemies become His footstool.

MISTAKE #10

Mistake #10: The failure of telling people of the demands of discipleship in following a crucified Savior. Rather, we paint salvation as all red roses and honey blossoms where your road will be smooth now that you are a believer. But Christ laid down His demands of discipleship very clearly in the Gospels. Jesus said, "Foxes have holes, and the birds of the air have nests; but the Son of man hath not where to lay his head" (Matthew 8:20). Jesus spoke about the demands of following Him" If any man will come after me, let him deny himself, and take up his cross, and follow me. For whosoever will save his life shall lose it: and whosoever will lose his life for my sake shall find it" (Matthew 16:24-25).

Becoming a Christian means life everlasting but it also means a present and daily death. Death to self, mortification of sin and self-denial.

"I am crucified with Christ: nevertheless I live; yet not I, but Christ liveth in me: and the life which I now live in the flesh I live by the faith of the Son of God who loved me; and gave himself for me" (Galatians 2:20).

These ten mistakes of modern evangelism have done much hurt to the church. We must faithfully preach the full counsel of God. We must preach the gospel in its purity and proper order. We must preach the great doctrines of ruin, redemption, repentance, and regeneration. We must warn sinners about a everlasting and burning hell that is prepared for all who die in their sins outside the blood of Christ Jesus. We must awaken a sinner to his lost condition before we present a remedy for sin. We must preach up the Lordship of Christ and show mankind the utter strictness and severity of God's holy law.

We must be honest with folks and tell them of the demands of discipleship in following Jesus.

Perhaps the next generation of young preachers will be better trained in these areas and preach the full counsel of God and warn men and women about their dangers of damnation and their great need of a Savior from sin in the Person of Christ Jesus.[16]

[16] Ibid, pp89-100.

ABOUT THE AUTHOR

E.A. Johnston in the Outdoor pulpit at Hanham Mount where George Whitefield preached, courtesy of Digby James.

E. A. Johnston, Ph.D., D. B. S., is a Fellow with the Stephen Olford Institute for Biblical Preaching and is an evangelist and author with eighteen published books. He is the founder of Evangelism Awakening, a revival-based ministry whose focus is the study of historical revival, and preaching for revival in our day. He has over two thousand sermons on SermonAudio.com.

SOME OF THE BOOKS BY E. A. JOHNSTON

Many of the following books may be purchased individually or as a set by going to Dr. Johnston's webpage in the bookstore at The Old Paths Publications that has links to distributors. Go to:

www.theoldpathspublications.com/Pages/ Authors/Johnston.htm

PLEASE NOTE THE "the" in the address

1. "A Heart Awake: The Authorized Biography of J. Sidlow Baxter" Foreword by Adrian Rogers (The Old Paths Publications, www.theoldpathspublications.com).

2. "Realities Of Revival" Foreword by Stephen F. Olford (Gospel Folio Press, Canada; 2005).

3. "No Turning Back" (Gospel Folio Press, Canada; 2005).

4. "The Master's Plan: Unfolding God's Blueprint For Your Life" (Gospel Folio Press, Canada; 2006).

5. "Know The Book: Bible Survey At A Glance" (Gospel Folio Press, Canada; 2007).

6. "Jua Kitabu: Tazamo la Biblia" Know The Book translated into the Swahili by missionary G. I. Harlow (Everyday Publications, Canada; 2007).

7. "Walking With God" Foreword by Ted S. Rendall (Gospel Folio Press, Canada; 2007).

8. "Return To Me: Entering A Right Relationship With God" (Gospel Folio Press, Canada; 2007).

9. "Are You In The Book Of Life?" (Gospel Folio Press, Canada; 2008).

10. "Call To Revival" Foreword By Colin Peckham (Gospel Folio Press, Canada; 2008).

11. "The Church In Revival" Foreword By Richard Owen Roberts (Gospel Folio Press, Canada; 2008).

12. "Olford On Scroggie: Stephen Olford's Notes on the Sermon Outlines of Graham Scroggie" Co-authored with Stephen Olford (The Old Paths Publications: www.theoldpathspublications.com).

13. "George Whitefield A Definitive Biography, Volumes 1 and 2 Combined" (The Old Paths Publications: www.theoldpathspublications.com).

14. "George Whitefield A Definitive Biography In Two Volumes" (American edition published by Revival Literature, Asheville; 2012).

15. "God's Hitchhike Evangelist The Biography Of Rolfe Barnard" Foreword By Bob Doom (The Old Paths Publications: www.theoldpathspublications.com).

16. "Asahel Nettleton Revival Preacher" Foreword By John Thornbury, Preface By Richard Owen Roberts (The Old Paths Publications: www.theoldpathspublications.com).

17. "Sermons For Revival" (The Old Paths Publications: www.theoldpathspublications.com).

18. "A Noble Company Biographical Essays on Notable Particular Baptists in America Volume 11: Portrait of Rolfe Barnard" (Particular Baptist Press, Springfield; 2018).

19. "Lectures On Revival For A Laodicean Church," (The Old Paths Publications, www.theoldpathspublications.com)

20. "Sam Jones, A New Biography" (The Old Paths Publications: www.theoldpathspublications.com)
21. E. A. Johnston's Book Set, (The Old Paths Publications, www.theoldpathspublications.com (30% off retail)